ST. LOUIS BLACK WOMEN'S
Quilting & Cuisine:
STORIES OF LOVE AND HOPE

Rev. Paulette Sankofa
Author and Curator

This book was made possible with support from the
Missouri Humanities Council

Published by Paulette Sankofa LLC Aging Well Renaissance
St. Louis, Missouri

St. Louis Black Women's Quilting & Cuisine:
STORIES OF LOVE AND HOPE

Copyright © 2024 by Dr. Paulette Sankofa
All rights reserved.

No part of this publication may be reproduced or transmitted in any form whatsoever, by photography or xerography, by broadcast or transmission, by translation into any kind of language, nor by recording electronically or any information storage and retrieval system or by any other means, without permission in writing from the author, except for brief use in excerpts articles and reviews.

Publisher: Paulette Sankofa LLC Aging Well Renaissance,
St. Louis, MO 63121.

FIRST EDITION

Book and Cover Design by Michael Evans, mevans@mevansvcd.com
Cover Art copyright © Andrea Kharizma Hughes

Library of Congress Cataloging-in-Publication Data

Identifiers: LCCN: Library of Congress Control Number: 2024908726
ISBN: 978-1-736588-60-4 (paperback)

DEDICATIONS

First, to my late parents, Luella and Walter Handley

~ And ~

To the many St. Louis women who shared their culinary gifts, and fabric artists who created quilts, both of which provided us with comfort, a sense of warmth, love, and hope for each new day.

~ And ~

My daughter and encourager, Dr. Tayala Tolefree

~ And ~

The late Cuesta Benberry and Faith Ringgold

ACKNOWLEDGEMENTS AND GRATITUDE

Creative Narrative Assistance by
Rev. Karla Frye, Ph.D.

Cover Artwork by
Andrea Kharizma Hughes

Interview Transcriptions by
Brianna Holden

Book & Cover Design by
Michael Evans

TABLE OF CONTENTS

06.....FORWARD

08.....PREFACE

12.....Ch 01   Doing Something with a Little Nothing: *Culinary and Other Creativity*
                                                                    Linda Jones

22.....Ch 02   The Fabric of Our Lives   Bridget Stegall

34.....Ch 03   A Love Affair with Fabric   Angee Turner

44.....Ch 04   Bitten by the Cooking Bug   Jetton Neal

52.....Ch 05   Spiritual Meditation: *A Tale of Quilting, Four Cousins, and a Family Legacy*
                         Janice Hawthorne Griffin   Barbara Huddleston
                         Brenda Huddleston   LaShell Livingston McGee

68.....Ch 06   Of Fascination, Fabrics, and Family   Pamela Coaxum

74.....Ch 07   Wow, She Makes Good Cakes!   Harriet Mucherson

84.....Ch 08   Food… It's a Family Thing   Sheryl Simmons

90.....Ch 09   Consistency and Clarity: *Through Fabric*   Edna Patterson Petty

96.....Ch 10   The Chicken Soup Lady   Patricia "Tish" Carroll

104...Ch 11   The Quilting Connection   Jenine Fitzpatrick

110...Ch 12   Preparing Something Special   Tracy Beavers

118...Ch 13   Eating Like Home: *A Celebration of the Food Traditions of My Homeland*
                                                        Selas Kidane

124...Ch 14   I am Weaving the Colorful Threads of My Life
               through Fabric Art and Cuisine   Paulette Sankofa

138...Ch 15   Collecting Memories: Now It's Your Turn Paulette Sankofa

FOREWORD
Marla Arna Jackson

The collaboration and friendship throughout the project inspired me to write this forward and share my thoughts on the profound impact of the St. Louis Black Women's Quilting and Cuisine: Stories of Love and Hope.

From the moment I first laid eyes on the vibrant and intricate quilts created by the women of PEACE Weaving Wholeness, I was captivated. Each stitch and patch seemed to hold within it a beautiful story of resilience, community, and the power of art to heal and empower.

Dr. Sankofa's dedication and passion for showcasing the talents and stories of Black women in St. Louis is evident throughout this book. She has deftly curated a collection of quilts and recipes that not only celebrate the creativity and skill of these women but also serve as a platform for sharing their narratives.

As an artist, I have always believed in the transformative power of creativity. But watching these women breathe life into their quilts, I realized just how profound that transformation can be. With every stitch, they were not only creating stunning works of art but also reclaiming their history, expressing their identity, and finding solace amidst the challenges faced by their community.

Through the art class I taught, I witnessed firsthand how quilting became a space for healing, growth, and connection. The women shared stories of their ancestors, their struggles, and their dreams, all while skillfully crafting their quilts. It was truly a testament to how art can serve as a conduit for expression, communication, and healing.

The recipes included in this book add another layer of richness and depth to the narratives presented. Food is often a gateway to memories and experiences, and the inclusion of traditional recipes passed down from generation to generation allows us to further immerse ourselves in the culture and lived experiences of these remarkable women.

As we leaf through the pages of this book, we are invited into a world filled with love, resilience, and hope. We are reminded of the power of art to transcend barriers, bridge divides, and bring people together. And most importantly, we are reminded of the importance of amplifying the voices and experiences of Black women, whose stories have often been overlooked or silenced.

I am honored to have been a part of this project and to have witnessed the incredible talent and spirit of the women featured in this book. Their quilts and recipes not only tell a story, but they also invite us to reflect on our journeys and how we can come together to create a more inclusive and compassionate world.

In writing this forward, I hope to convey my deep admiration for the St. Louis Black Women's Quilting and Cuisine: Stories of Love and Hope and to encourage readers to approach these pages with an open heart and a willingness to learn, be inspired, and perhaps even challenge their perspectives.

May this book serve as a testament to the power of art, community, and the untold stories that weave through our lives. May it remind us all of the importance of embracing diversity, celebrating our shared humanity, and striving for a future filled with love and hope.

PREFACE
Rev. Paulette Sankofa

Quilting has long been a significant cultural and artistic practice among Black communities, serving as a means of storytelling, community building, and creative expression. The history of Black women's quilting in Missouri is rich and deeply rooted in both Black and American quilting traditions.

In Missouri, as in many other parts of the United States, Black women have used quilting as a way to preserve their cultural heritage, pass down traditions, and create beautiful and functional works of art. During slavery, quilting was often a communal activity, with women coming together to create quilts that served both practical and symbolic purposes.

One of the most notable aspects of Black women's quilting history in Missouri is the use of quilts as a form of communication on the Underground Railroad. Quilts were hung outside or displayed in specific ways to convey messages to escaping slaves, providing them with valuable information and guidance on their journey to freedom.

In more recent times, Black women in Missouri have continued the tradition of quilting, blending traditional techniques with modern styles and themes. Quilting remains an important art form and cultural practice, reflecting the resilience, creativity, and cultural heritage of Black women in Missouri and beyond.

Cuesta Benberry (1923–2007) was a pioneering researcher, writer, and historian known for her groundbreaking work on Black quilting and quilt makers. She played a significant role in bringing attention to the contributions of Black quilt makers to the American quilting tradition.

Born in St. Louis, Missouri, Cuesta developed an early interest in quilting, which eventually led her to become one of the foremost authorities on the subject. In the 1960s, at a time when Black contributions to quilting were largely overlooked, Cuesta began researching and documenting the history of Black quilting.

Her research culminated in the publication of several influential books and articles, including "Always There: The African-American Presence in American Quilts" (1992) and "Piecework: The Magazine of Needlework and Textiles," where she served as a contributing editor for x number of years.

Cuesta's work helped to highlight the significance of quilting in Black culture, showcasing the artistry, creativity, and cultural heritage of Black quilt makers. Her efforts have contributed to a greater understanding and appreciation of Black quilting traditions and have inspired generations of quilters and historians.

In a 2007 article in the St. Louis American, she spoke of her journey from her early understanding of the Black quilting art form that she was introduced to through her husband's family in Grand Rivers, Kentucky. "I thought I knew what a quilt was—a blanket!... I had never seen quilts like theirs. They called them by the pattern names; they might say, 'This is my Catch as Catch Can' or 'my Sugar Bowl.' And they were so proud."

Cuesta went on to become a renowned historian, and passionate scholar on Black quilting traditions, their importance in the narrative of the United States, and global knowledge of our quilting traditions. She was quoted as saying she had been "gathering patterns, blocks of fabric, and remnants of memory that would change the world's understanding of African-American quilts."

The connection between quilting and cuisine in Black culture is deeply rooted in history and has played a significant role in the Civil Rights movement. Both quilting and cuisine have been vital forms of expression, storytelling, and community building for Blacks.

There are historical roots. Quilting and cuisine have been integral parts of Black culture since the time of slavery. Just as enslaved Blacks used quilting as a means of artistic expression, often incorporating African textile traditions into their quilts, similarly, cuisine was a way for enslaved individuals to preserve cultural traditions and create dishes from limited resources.

There is community and identity. Quilting circles and communal kitchens were important spaces for Blacks to come together, share stories, and pass down traditions. These practices helped to strengthen community bonds and preserve cultural identity. There are connections to the Civil Rights Movement. During the Civil Rights movement, quilting and cuisine continued to play important roles. Quilts were used as symbols of resistance and solidarity, with some quilts containing hidden messages and symbols related to the movement. Additionally, communal meals and food-sharing were central to organizing efforts and provided a sense of unity and strength among activists.

There is cultural preservation. Both quilting and cuisine have been important tools for preserving Black culture. Through quilting, stories, and traditions are stitched into fabric, while cuisine keeps ancestral flavors and cooking techniques alive.

And then there's artistic expression. In addition to their cultural significance, quilting and cuisine have also been forms of artistic expression for Blacks. Quilts and dishes are often crafted with meticulous care and attention to detail, showcasing the creativity and skill of the makers.

Overall, the connection between quilting and cuisine in Black culture is a testament to the resilience, creativity, and cultural richness of Black communities. These traditions continue to be celebrated and honored as important aspects of Black heritage.

In 1993, the National Council of Negro Women released The Black Family Dinner Quilt Cookbook, featuring Dorothy Height as its editor. Dorothy Height, a prominent figure in women's and Black Civil Rights activism, was instrumental in bringing this project to fruition. The cookbook was a celebration of quilting, culinary arts, and their profound ties to the history of Black people. It emphasized the importance of these traditions in Black culture and family life, showcasing their enduring significance and contribution to the cultural tapestry of African American heritage.

Interviews for this book began at the beginning of the COVID-19 pandemic in 2020, and that period is reflected in some of the stories. It has been a journey of an ongoing commitment to its completion and an understanding of the importance of documenting the stories that have kept me going.

These women shared their passion for creating food and quilts that are not only gifts for their families and friends but also embodiments of a rich cultural history. St. Louis Black Women's Quilting and Cuisine: Stories of Love and Hope, is a beautiful exploration through personal stories of how quilting and cuisine serve as forms of art, cultural preservation, and expressions of love and hope within the community.

Linda Jones

DOING SOMETHING WITH A LITTLE OF NOTHING: CULINARY AND OTHER CREATIVITY

Chapter One

"I had my grandmother, my great grandmother, my mom, my paternal grandmother, all these women who gave me background or inspiration or showed me how to do something with a little of nothing."

There is a common thread in these stories, one that speaks of creativity, beauty and art. And also stories beyond those of quilts and cobbler and collards. The intergenerational threads of faith, strength, hope, wisdom and more are woven through the stories of mothers and foremothers who passed down decades of knowledge, tenacity and spirit rooted in love.

Through the skills and creativity shared in their chapters of these generations-long stories, the women in this collection offer images of perseverance repeated in similar lives with a variety of diverse patterns, pans, and pots across this country.

Linda Jones' story connects with others here in a visible, palpable way, allowing readers to see them in the way she carves those images in bas relief – connected in the background, but reaching out just enough to create a unique personal connection. Her laid-back demeanor evokes the truth that lies in memory and storytelling, while her laugh, smiles, and simplicity of language finishes the job. Linda's story is emblematic of a shared experience, which although diverse, resonates across contributors and hopefully, with readers. Whether she speaks of her grandmother's creative quilts or incredible cobbler, Linda glows with the joy of one whose personality and life path have been greatly influenced, infiltrated, and molded by women who express their love and life's lessons through the art and practice of creating: cooking, gardening, quilting, sewing, and other forms through which the essence of their beings breathe, giving life to others.

Linda is a self-described creative spirit who "started young," explaining that she "enjoyed arts and crafts when [I] was a girl. I enjoyed writing when I was a girl... I started writing poetry. And also in college I started making silver jewelry." A long line of women -grandmothers on both sides of her family, a great grandmother, and her mother - inspired her creativity and resourcefulness, fostering an ability to "do something with a little of nothing." She recalls her great-grandmother repurposing old socks, "rolling them in a certain way" to make soft balls so that grandchildren visiting on the weekend could throw a soft ball around the house." Smiling as she reminisced, "she was ok with that and would make the soft ball for us. She was just good with things like that…" Linda's great-grandmother also gave Linda a gift that would keep giving long after her passing away, teaching her as a young girl how to lay down a crust just so for peach cobbler, deftly spooning the fruit into the pan to avoid splashing.

That attention to detail and a knack for combining ingredients into amazing combinations of form and flavor is a legacy that Linda carries on in her own rendition of the blackberry cobbler as her great-grandmother taught her. Linda's own touch builds on the tradition of using what is at hand and adds the delight of discovery that, in the way of true cooks, adds a personal twist. For instance, she recounts, "…how we would make cobbler out of canned fruit", as she remembers learning from her grandmother as they cooked together, adding, "but then eventually I found out fresh blackberries have a lighter and more rich color and I stopped using the canned ones and I started using the fresh ones," sometimes freezing the berries for later use.

The little how-to knack for making things that Linda learned from the women in her life extended outward from the matrilineal lines of mother and grandmothers to other women in her life. Linda fondly shakes her head as she says, "then there are the aunties…I had an aunt in Chicago who made me a necklace when I was in college –in her senior citizen class, something like classes that were offered by a local nonprofit, PEACE Weaving Wholeness– with teeny tiny beads, all of these beads threaded into a beautiful necklace with matching earrings. She taught me as a high school senior that 'you are still special in my life and I have something special for you." Linda had the necklace for over 30 years until it broke about two years ago, but for three decades that gift consistently conveyed its message, subtly signifying its importance. "I wore it for a long time and gave it a good wear."

Linda understands all these influences as markers of what she calls 'basics of her personality.' Her life story sounds typical, until she uses its surface commonality as a powerful conduit, a connecting of forces that weaves in details and stirs up similarities that bring shared experience to life. Born and raised in St. Louis, Linda's creativity, love of music, and educational foundation were fueled by that historic city's geographic centrality, race relations, and the migratory experience of its African American community. After college, Linda committed her professional life to sharing her knowledge and experience working on college campuses, with the Girl Scouts, and in "inner city urban programs for girls". "So all of my interests and even my professional interests have been trying to make life better for others, for families, and the community. And I am still trying to do that now through my art and my writings. I'm trying to leave a legacy to make our community better and to inspire and enrich others."

Linda's perception of the 'circle of life' centers on the idea that one can use memories and stories of the past to fuel herself and others in the present, leaving a legacy for those who come after. This Sankofa-esque practice of looking to one's past to inform one's present, reinforces that all lessons – simple, complex and those in between – are useful. We gain much as we discover that extracting their life-giving essence ensures that a meaningful legacy continues.

Linda remembers that her mother cooked a full meal every day, replete with cornbread and Kool-Aid. ® And on Sundays, Linda describes, "she would cook a hen or make a bigger version of Sunday dinner. Sunday dinners were like at 'Big Mamas'. Two meats or three or four sides and it was nice." Linda spent many days as a little girl in the kitchen with her mother and great grandmother Sally Young, who did the desserts and biscuits. It is she who taught Linda to bake, "especially with crust because my mother didn't do a lot with crust," Linda explained. "She was a big cake maker. So I was there helping with her pound cakes and Swans Down three layer cakes, coconut pineapple, chocolate, lemon, strawberry, cherry, you name it." Linda's high school home economics teacher recognized her cooking skills, and as early as her sophomore year, Linda helped her with large cooking projects. Linda attributes her abilities to genetics as well as the early instruction from highly skilled women when she shares, "my father was a chef and he started cooking at a young age when he was a boy. My dad was an executive chef so it's in the blood."

Although not as avid a cook as Jones' paternal grandmother and great grandmother, her maternal grandmother lived next door and would sometimes contribute to family gatherings. The warmth of cooking with her elders helped define family. "It was family…if it was a holiday, like Memorial Day coming up or Fourth of July or whatever, we would all come together and BBQ and make the side dishes and put on some music and they would play cards afterward and it was always a coming together of family." The undertones of those gathering is strong, and the absence of their inherent bond of love bothers Jones, who misses the "coming together" that was so natural in her younger years. Jones' feelings are exacerbated by age and distance, among other things. She explains that "…now that I'm in my late 60s, I see that I am at that pendulum [point] where they were. The younger people in our family live out of town now so we have to communicate in other ways…that's why I am trying to leave the legacy now through different avenues. Anytime that we can teach and pass on these nuggets, I think that it is important that people know our history, our foundation, and move forward from that and take it to the next level.

Where cooking conveys vibrancy and motion in Jones' life, her artwork was something she "did for quiet time," she says. "Even now I like to do my artwork for when I am quiet and still. It seems like it is calming and soothing." As a lifelong lover of shapes and colors, Jones' recalls making abstract drawings during free time in school using a black crayon on Manila paper to draw shapes to then color. It's a technique she applies today in some of her abstract pieces using acrylic and watercolors and acrylic paint sticks in place of crayons. "And there is something about those colors [that] draw me, even in flowers and clothing, and just different things, color just draws me - bright colors, pinks and yellows and blues and greens and orange and red. I just love those colors."

Like cooking, Linda was drawn to art, but this time, she was attracted by a work-study job during her sophomore year in college in which she had an opportunity to create jewelry. This was an opportunity that bore fruit much later, when Linda became ill a few years ago and was diagnosed with thyroid cancer.… When she was about to start radiation treatments, Linda said, she was nervous, "and I just felt I needed to do something that would calm me down. If I would take this painting class somebody was telling me about, then maybe this class would help me, I said, because I need something to go through this period of my life to keep my confidence up and my faith up and just keep me up." The class, designed for children, and from which she graduated calmed Linda and more, leading to a pastime that became a passion. After gaining interest in her art from others in her church and community, Linda entered shows and received recognition and a few awards. Inspired, Linda says she "started painting these ladies, similar to me with neck issues from the thyroid and people started calling them 'my sister girls' and 'long neck ladies' and I was pouring out what was happening internally onto my canvas, so art was healing. Art was comforting. It gave me some pleasure and relaxation, and it was inspirational to others".

Understanding her art's true sources, Linda is always connecting her creativity and its relationship and value to the community. Even when asked about a quilt she has that belonged to her grandmother, Linda talks about the quilt in terms of family and community, touches on history and its moments, weaving an engaging story of her family's migratory history and her desire to refurbish the quilt made of images of tiny postage stamps. There were other quilts in the family but after moving several times, many were taken or lost…"so I think I have one of the last family quilts that was made in Henning, Tennessee."

Bringing the conversation full circle, Linda effortlessly connects several dates and places in African American history at a level we can all understand and relate to, calling on our roots, rituals, and relationships to identify and affirm who we are. "My mother's side, my maternal side is from Henning Tennessee, the same place where Alex Haley's parents and grandparents were from. Not that far from Memphis… I used to go down to Knoxville to the Haley farm when we had our St. Louis Freedom School at Jamison Church in the late 1990s and early 2000s."

Linda talks about her family in the context of a historical moment, knowing that these facts give meaning to her life and to those connected to her by blood and community kinship. This rich and layered conversation offers visual snapshots linking together the living color life of a multifaceted community gem. One of many like herself, each story Linda shares is a page that bring to life common experiences and traditions among diverse people. Her story affirms

Linda's place in a tightly knit family surrounded by community. As she speaks of a life grounded in history, tenacity and culture, those who listen find their place, as well.

Every weekend, Linda posts photos of her Sunday dinner on Facebook. Everything looks absolutely scrumptious. She decided to share her recipe for Mac and Cheese.

SOULFUL MACARONI & CHEESE

Ingredients:
- ½ of a 16-ounce box of Creamettes Large Elbow Macaroni Noodles (Boiled and drained)
- 8-ounce Package of Velveeta Cheese
- ½ to ¾ can of Milnot Condensed Milk
- ½ cup Whole Milk
- 1 stick of butter
- 2 teaspoons of black pepper
- 1 teaspoon of paprika
- 1 Egg slightly beaten
- 2 cups of shredded sharp cheddar cheese
- 1 cup of shredded gouda cheese
- ½ cup of Colby or other melting cheese

Preparation:
1. Lightly grease a 10-12-inch ceramic baking dish.
2. Preheat oven to 350 degrees.
3. In a large 2-quart pan on low heat melt Velveeta, butter and add Milnot.
4. Then add a slightly beaten egg, milk and 1 cup of cheddar cheese, 1 cup of gouda cheese and the ½ cup of Colby or your choice. Save 1 cup of shredded cheddar cheese to put on the top of your dish.
5. Stir mixture well and add cooked macaroni.
6. Add seasonings, pepper and paprika and stir all well.
7. Pour mixture into the baking dish and sprinkle the remaining cheddar cheese on top.
8. Bake for 40 – 50 minutes until a light golden brown.
9. Serve and enjoy!

Clockwise from far left:

Patchwork Quilt
Gramama Sallie Walker Young,
Handmade Quilt

Cotton
Lynda Jones
Painting

Peach Cobbler Party
Lynda Jones
Painting

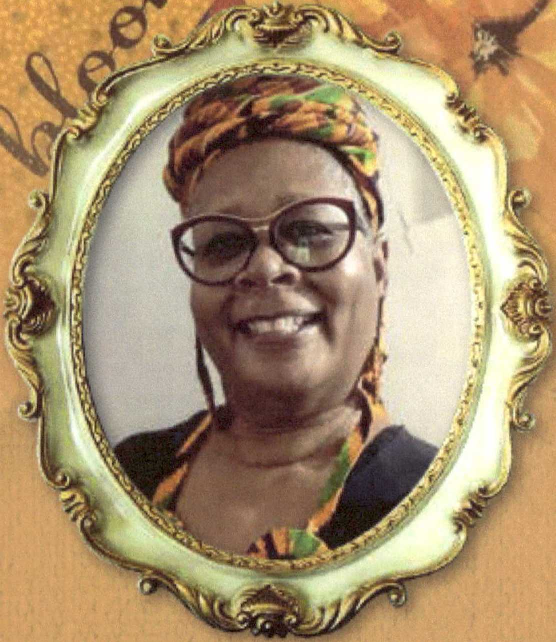

Bridget Ford Stegall

THE FABRIC OF OUR LIVES

"Who knew that the journey of sistah-hood and skill building in Kansas, would lead to lasting friendships and a new world of artistic opportunities?"

Bridget Ford Stegall traveled an interesting path to becoming a fabric artist. She graduated from SIU in Edwardsville with a degree in Elementary Education. She says she knew it was her calling since she was a little girl playing school on her front porch.

When she graduated from SIU-E, she was given the opportunity to work for the local telephone company. There she worked in their engineering department, and remained there for about 20 years. Eventually, there was a large company layoff which had her wondering what she would do next. "I knew that my passion was to teach, but it took me a couple of years of working for Lucent Technologies to decide that I needed to follow my true calling. I needed a purpose." She applied to St. Louis Public Schools to be an elementary education teacher. She ultimately did that for 19 years. She taught grades from kindergarten, third to eighth. She felt the best thing about her time teaching was that she stayed at the same school, Peabody Elementary, which allowed her to make a great connection with the community.

Bridget's experience with working with computers at the telephone company opened the door to a computer-based program offered to the teachers. The eMints program introduced teachers to education based programs and websites. After her two year training she was asked to teach the next group of teachers.

Even though fabric art wasn't part of her professional career, up to that point, Bridget had a history with, and a passion for, sewing. Her grandmother was a seamstress, and her mom also sewed. "My mom often tells a story of how she and my grandmother couldn't afford to go to the department stores and just buy things off the rack." So she, and my grandmother would go downtown and go into some of the stores to shop. Bridget's grandmother would ask her mom if she saw something she liked.

Then her grandmother would examine the dress or suit, checking the seams, lining, and general construction and then she would go home and create a pattern and make that outfit. "My grandmother even did that same thing for me. I showed her something in a magazine one time, and she created the jumper for me."

Bridget would watch her mom sew. Her mom made clothes for herself and for Bridget. Bridget fondly remembers a purple dress that her mother made for herself, and she made a matching one for Bridget. It was so cute, and she was so proud to be wearing a dress that matched her mom's.

When Bridget was about 14, she must have expressed that she wanted to learn to sew. She had sewn a gingham skirt by hand, but felt she was ready to learn to sew on the sewing machine. "I'm not sure exactly what the conversation was but that Christmas there was an Easy Sew pattern under the tree along with some cream colored, large well corduroy fabric." She learned to lay and cut the fabric mostly by reading the pattern directions and guidance from her mother and then sewed it on her Mom's black metal Singer sewing machine. She fondly remembers that was her most cherished Christmas present that year.

Bridget sewed mostly for herself but, every once in a while she sewed gifts for others. Things changed when she had children. She has two daughters, and a son. She began to sew for them. It was not only something practical for her to do, it was also a gift of love.

Every Easter Saturday, she would be up into the wee hours finishing her daughters' Easter dresses. Every once-in-a-while, she would also make an outfit for her son. As her children grew older "they didn't want my Easter dresses", instead she put her expressions of creativity and love in sewing their Prom dresses.

Then one year, her son was ready to go to his first high school prom. He asked her to make a suit for him. Bridget was nervous. Men's clothing was a little more difficult. She had tried in the past but had not been successful. But she thought "Hey, I had made dresses for the girls and so I was determined to make a suit for him." She and her son chose a pattern, and then he said he wanted it to be made of denim. Bridget thought,

"Western"? The pattern wasn't western and denim wasn't really prom wear. He wanted a three-piece suit but just out of denim. His girlfriend was going to wear a denim dress. Bridget says she was so proud of the outcome. It was very nice. From that experience, Bridget became so confident that she agreed to and sewed her youngest daughter's wedding dress.

It wasn't immediate that Bridget moved from sewing clothing to other types of creative work with fabric. In July of 2019, there was a summer camp for Seasoned Older Adults, sponsored by Peace Weaving Wholeness. Quilting was one of the classes. Bridget joined the quilting class. "I had watched my grandmother quilt, but my grandmother mostly hand-quilted. She'd have this big quilting hoop in her bedroom, and she'd be sitting in her rocking chair quilting while she watched one of her shows. We still have some of those quilts." While Bridget was fascinated by the process, she also found it a bit daunting. She said "It looked like a lot of work and even though the quilts her grandmother made were beautiful, I wasn't sure I wanted to be challenged in that way." Taking the quilting class showed her that she could use a sewing machine to quilt. To her surprise, quilting was not hard at all. She felt that since she already knew how to use a sewing machine, she could have some level of confidence, and was open to the world of quilting and mixed media art.

Up to this point, Bridget had never thought of herself as an artist. She didn't know how to paint or draw, and had never considered the idea that she could be a fabric artist. But a fabric artist was in her. After the camp ended a group of the quilting class participants, now known as the STL Quilting Queens, traveled to Lawrence, Kansas to learn how to make portrait art quilts from quilting artist, activist, and historian, Marla Arna Jackson. As a matter of fact, the first project Bridget completed from that class, was a quilted portrait of her granddaughter. Who knew that the journey of sistah-hood and skill building in Kansas, would lead to lasting friendships and a new world of artistic opportunities?

Doors indeed opened for her. "That was just eye-opening to me, and it afforded the opportunity to be creative in other ways, as well." Because of her artistic skills, previous experience teaching, and spirit of love and community building, she was recruited to be an instructor with Peace Weaving Wholeness.

Bridget has a real passion for teaching fabric art, but she is equally passionate about genealogy research. She was asked if she could put all of these together and teach a class where the participants could research their family and create a piece of art from their findings. She was always in awe at how creative her students were. She had several participants who would say, "I'm not an artist" or " I don't know how to do this". But her teaching style is very student-centered. She says "I'm really one of those teachers who shows examples but never wants you to make something exactly like everyone else makes. The most creative art comes from this method."

Bridget says she has bins and bins of fabric. She loves the many colors and textures. Originally, she bought fabric for an individual outfit or two, but now has fabric for future projects, or at least her children hope that it's for future projects. Right now, her focus is African prints that she likes to incorporate into her quilts and in her other fabric art. For her virtual classes, she creates a package of supplies for each participant. She is always intentional to include pieces of African fabric. That way each person can decide if they want to include it in their individual creation.

When Bridget reflects on what art she wants to create in the future, she thinks about new and innovative ways she can use fabric. "I've taken a few online classes. I want to explore working more with patterned fabric and coordinating colors." She's been watching YouTube videos and joining different online organizations to see how she can make that happen.

She's excited that she is now a professional artist. "Yes, I'm an official artist now." She had submitted three of her quilt pieces for an exhibit at the Zuka Gallery in the Old North Neighborhood of St Louis. Her piece Warrior Woman was hanging in the 14th Street Art Gallery for a few weeks. She wasn't around to try to sell it. As a matter of fact, she was out-of-town most of that time. "Now, I've been to a lot of art exhibits and art shows and, you know, the artist is usually there and they're talking about their art. But my art was just hanging there. I had not even thought of the idea of selling it." Then, one day, she got an email from the exhibit curator, Andrea Hughes, saying that someone was interested in buying one of my pieces. Bridget says she was in shock. "I'd never thought of selling my art and had no way of knowing the logistics of it." She reached out to a couple of seasoned artists to help determine how to set a price, and it was sold to a woman who collected African influenced art. Bridget said that was an amazing experience.

This year Bridget presented on the history of quilting, with an emphasis on African American quilts and art quilts, at the St Louis Art Museum.

She looked back over her journey emerging as an artist and thought about the process. She had not been an artist. She had been a retiree from non-arts-based careers. And now five years later, she has started selling her creations. She shares, "I'm still blown away." She believes there's much more to come.

Angee Turner

A LOVE AFFAIR WITH FABRIC

Chapter Three

> *"Angee Turner is an award winning quilt maker, designer, and teacher. She has been sewing since childhood and began quilting over 20 years ago. Her quilts hang on walls and lie on beds in private collections across the country."*

Angee Turner did not intend to become a quilt maker. Her mother and grandmother taught her to sew when she was a child. In fact, her mother said "Sew or be naked" because she went to Catholic school and each child needed 6 uniform shirts, and 2 jumpers. That is what you wore every day. "I didn't have a lot of clothes. I had hand me downs." So in order to wear the cute clothes Angee wanted to wear, she had to sew.

So she spent her whole life sewing and had all these scraps in a bucket and her father's mother, her paternal grandmother, was a quilt maker but she lived in Michigan and she didn't know her that much. "Every couple of years I used to get a quilt from her in the mail for my birthday. It was usually wrapped in a grocery store bag with some white string tied around it. So I had collected all these quilts over the years and I had one on my bed that had started to fray and had hand stitched it here and there and patched it here and there." One day Angee thought "maybe I'll take those scraps underneath my table and redo my grandma's quilt and all I knew is you take those squares and you sew them together." That's all she knew.

So she set out sewing these four patches together and before she knew it, she had made a little quilt. "I think I had it on the table and then it became my cats' little space to sit." She then took some more squares and her second quilt was just about king sized, not on purpose, but "we had a snow day for school and I just sewed until we were out of squares." She went to a quilt shop and the lady told her how to sew on the sashing and whatever else. "I made a quilt and after that thought 'oh that's kind of fun'." Excited by that, she got some books from the library, and before she knew it she just started replicating what she saw. From there, she became obsessed.

Angee talks about her love of fondling fabric. She laments about the fact that folks in St. Louis don't have good fabric stores anymore. "Twenty, 30 years ago we had different options for fabric stores." There were So-Fro Fabrics and Fabric Warehouse that became Hand Cut, then there were independent stores like Winston's fabrics, and there was Eunice Farmer so there were lots of choices to choose from. "Today, we really only have Jackman's but Jackman's has become primarily a quilting store where it was known to have beautiful wedding fabrics as well. They also had beautiful woolens. They are now primarily a quilting store because much of the fabric stores have become crafty. Even if you go to Joanne's, which had been a fabric store, it is now really a craft store that sells fabric. I love fabric, I love the colors, the patterns, the feel of cottons because I primarily use cottons. I just love everything about it. I love the smell of it, and all that stuff."

When Angee is creating, she draws on her love of fabric and lots of ideas. "I'm always very observant of where I am especially if I go someplace new." She is the person who looks at the floor. "You know, what's the pattern on the floor? Or in the bathroom. What's the tiling in the bathroom?" She is always looking for patterns she hasn't seen before. So she collects photographs of things, and keeps a collection for reference. Anything that attracts her attention. Things like color combinations. For example, if there is a color combination that she hasn't seen before she will find that interesting. "I tend to look at nature blogs, National Geographic and look at the animals… you know birds have beautiful coloring, just the color combinations… so I am very open to what I see around me and I keep notebooks." She has notebooks of patterns that she drew from 15-20 years ago so sometimes she goes back and looks through them. Sometimes she might make something today, and then go back to look at the notebook and that is something she drew a long time ago and it popped into her head. She reflects that "oh that idea is from 15 years ago, but something triggers it."

Her creative process is daily and she has to do something creative every day. She sews something…"sometimes I don't have time so it's just one seam. But I set up my studio so that I am always prepared to do something." There is always something on the table that is available for her to work on. There is something by the sewing machine so there is something to work on. Angee has a process her work, and her process is her practice. Some things you all see and some things you don't. Sometimes the practice is not to complete something, sometimes it is just working out an idea. "Is this color combo going to work? Oooo I don't think that it's going to work." But she feels that it might teach her something that she will use in another project.

Angee compares it to the discipline of dancing. "Yes, it's like a ballerina. Even though you are a prima ballerina you still go to class every day. But that's keeping the muscles ready. When you get that idea like 'Oh I've got this idea' then it's easier when I get home to just get the fabric and work on it because I have that confidence from practicing every day."

She reflects on the fact that she took her work for granted for a long time. "I knew I was good but it was just me… I was making things, and I was making pretty things and it was just what I do and my creative outlet." It wasn't until she was invited to show her work at the Jacoby Arts Center in Alton where she thought "You want me to exhibit? Like really?" And she thought "wow someone else is seeing something that I'm not seeing then."

So when she began hanging the quilts… first of all she realized she didn't know how to hang or organize them, so she reached out to a couple people and asked for help. The mathematician in her cut out photos of the quilts and laid them out to organize them for a 40-foot wall. She got a 0-inch piece of paper and made scale size versions of each quilt. There were 8 quilts that she hung. And once she put them up on the wall, and took a step back, "it made me cry. It made me cry because I thought, wow this is saying something about me… and it made me think about how women… Black women in particular in that we take ourselves for granted." She thought about how we take our nurturing for granted. "We take the work that we do for granted. We take our creativity for granted. You never step back and say "Damn, I'm pretty damn good, and it's ok to do that."

Sometimes we, as Black women, are taught that that's being egotistical or we should be humble. Angie remembered Maya Angelou talked about "forget that humbleness mess". "Basically Angelou was saying that being humble is bullshit. If you have a talent and a skill and an ability and you are sharing that with the world, that is God's gift to you and you have that right to be sure of that and feel good about that within yourself. Don't say… 'ohhh it's not that great… or it's not as good as another person'. You accept and say thank you. It is pretty damn good isn't it?" She said there are some quilts that are 'eh it's ok' and other quilts that she can say "damn girl you really put your foot in that one… that was really good" and she quipped, "I can say that to myself, but I can also say to my sister girl… 'girl that quilt you made was fire'."

Angee believes that feeling good about herself and her work does not prevent her from saying to someone else "damn that was good". She appreciates and understands what it takes to do something and show it to the world and say "this is mine". She tries to encourage other women to be bold and let the light shine on you because for so long she was told "don't let the light shine on you… be in the background." She now declares "No!" She appreciates it when she is called a Master Quilter, because she sees herself as on her way to being there. But she also wants to bring someone else along too and say "Oh thank you for the attention you're giving me but do you also see my sister over here or my brother over there. I think there is room enough for everybody."

Angee talks about her approach to teaching. She wants people to enjoy it, and has different approaches for different groups. "I tell you it depends on the group of people. If they are real beginners and they don't know anything, I want them to enjoy it and want to continue. If it is someone who has experience already and they may have quilted before and they want to learn something, I want them to enjoy it and learn something." She really wants them to learn something new. She is also open to the possibility that they will teach her something that she didn't know. Or maybe teach her a different way of doing something.

Her biggest message to people is just make it. "Just make it!" On Instagram she did a screen shot once that said every quilt does not have to be beautiful. "I think that people think 'oh my quilt isn't as beautiful, and my stitches aren't as nice as yours'." But she says her first quilt was janky… she didn't know what in the world she was doing but she finished it. So she tells people just finish it. "You don't have to put a picture on Facebook or Instagram. Just finish it. That quilt may be your first quilt that your baby crawls on and spits up on. Or it may be the quilt you crawl up under if you've had a bad day at work and you know you just want to lay on the couch and cry. Just make the quilt and finish it. In making it you are going to learn something. You are going to learn what you can do, what you can't, or want to never do again. You are going to learn something with every quilt you make."

"Just like anything you are making you practice, you try something and you practice, practice practice. Nothing that you do creatively… when you are starting… is going to be your best. But the more you do it, the better you get. You just have to continue. Just try it. And if quilting is not for you, maybe something else is. It could be knitting, embroidery, or macramé." Angee says she used to tell people "Just make something" because we shouldn't spend our whole lives just being consumers. Make something! She plans to be 116 years old with stacks and stacks of quilts. She doesn't have children so all she has to leave behind in the world are children that she has taught and quilts that she has made. "So just make stuff because in the future, it is the things that we have made that people will study and that will tell the story of who we were as human beings. So just make stuff."

And she's trying to learn new things herself, because she knows how to quilt. She took a class cutting out fabric and gluing it kind of like applique. It made her think differently about how to add that to her practice. She's also seen beautiful bead work and stitching and all that. And she thinks

"I'm gonna try that!" She thinks that maybe she will try to add that to some quilts. She's trying to add some texture to her work… and going back to some of the sewing and tailoring skills that she knows and incorporating that into her work.

Teaching opens her up to things that other people do, and how she can add that to her practice. She believes it's all about practice. It's about the practice and the process and the finished quilt is the cherry on top. It is the result of her practice, but the practice and the process are even more important than the finished item. Angee reflected back on the COVID-19 pandemic a few years ago and how people got into journaling and quilting. People went through so many emotions during that time. Fortunately, she had materials around so she was productive.

"You know the one thing this pandemic has taught me was if you want to do something, just do it now. There is no use sitting around waiting for things when you could just do it in the moment. If you want to give people things, might as well do it while you're around to see them use it and if they're done using it, throw it away." She's purchased a long-arm quilting machine which has greatly expanded her quilting options, and her practices. She says all she has in her house is quilts and books and more books, so she flipped her house and uses it the way she wants to. "Why am I waiting to use all my things? Who am I waiting for? I'm not saving stuff for somebody else. I'm gonna use it while I'm here." And that she does in making remarkably, beautiful, quilts that reflect her sense of creativity and commitment to her craft.

Angee also expresses her creative spirit through culinary arts. She has chosen to share the following recipe which is one of her favorites.

SWEET POTATO BREAD WITH PECANS

Ingredients
- 2-1/3 cups sugar
- 2/3 cup water
- 2/3 cup oil
- 4 eggs
- 2 cups mashed sweet potatoes
- 3-1/3 cups flour
- 2 tsp baking soda
- 1-1/2 tsp salt
- 1/2 tsp cinnamon
- 1/2 tsp baking powder
- 1 cup chopped pecans

Preparation
1. Heat oven to 350 degrees.
2. Combine sugar, water, eggs, and sweet potatoes. Mix thoroughly.
3. Add dry ingredients.
4. Add pecans.
5. Divide between two greased loaf pans and bake 50 minutes.
6. Cool in pan to room temperature before serving.

Jetton Neal

BITTEN BY THE COOKING BUG

Chapter Four

The cooking love bug may not have bitten her siblings, but for Jetton Neal, the fourth born of six children it's bite was early and made a lasting mark. Hers is a story of faith and joy that stirred a lifelong love of the culinary arts.

The taste of Jetton's food tells it all. She only knows one kind of cooking and baking, "from scratch". It's a term that has gained renewed use and the attention of newfound adherents, but its meaning and significance was never lost to some. And that includes Jetton. Combine what must have been an inborn desire to prepare and share meals with others with a cooking father who didn't hesitate to share all he knew with his baby girl, and you have a purist whose baking surpasses the norm.

It began with a child's idea of a picnic with cousins – the three of them led by Jetton, earnestly preparing a meal from scratch to be enjoyed later on the grounds of a landmark hospital where they had all been born, just across the street from their home. Although at five years of age, no fire was involved, Jetton already knew her way around the kitchen. Using what they had on hand: bread (using a precise six pieces, being sure to leave some for the family's dinner); mustard. Mayonnaise, and sugar. "We decided to have a picnic in the park… well we called it a park… actually it was the grounds of Homer G. Phillips Hospital, up under their trees."

As the eldest of the three, Jetton was the cook. She recounts the precision and attention to detail that would become a hallmark of her cooking and baking: "I made a mustard sandwich and I made a mayo sandwich and of course we needed a dessert so I made a sugar sandwich and they were all cut in threes." Armed with the square tin lunch boxes and canteens of the period, the three cousin-best friends marched "right across the street and sat on the street up under the tree," firmly establishing a culinary love and creating a memory that would last a lifetime. This early memory is filled with charm and the inkling of the birth of a culinary queen, but this cook's lifelong passion sprang into formation a few years later with a simple request to her father. "Daddy, can you teach me how to cook?"

As Jetton's mother was a nurse at another hospital, her father did most of the family's cooking. The sight and good smell of the smoke and steam captured an eight year-old's senses. When asked, Jetton's father replied "you want to learn how to cook?" perhaps amazed that his thin, short little girl was interested in tackling the challenge of cooking. Jetton recalls being unable to completely see "all the way over the counter" so her father would push a small stool right next to the stove allowing her to stand and watch him cook. "The first thing he told me to do before cooking was how to clean every meat that was brought into our home and after that he told me how to use the oven temperatures and how to gauge the top of the [gas] stove."

When those lessons were mastered, Jetton began to help him with preparing the meals. She says "That's when I knew that I wanted to cook. You know cooking is what I've always wanted to do. I've done a number of other things throughout my life, but I really enjoy cooking the most."

The story of Jetton's joy in cooking that began as a child, simmered in her being throughout the years, and became a dream come true later in life as a seasoned adult. I've started 'Abeela Sweets U Remember'. It's the name of a business that I created for myself, and I bake homemade cakes and pies from scratch.

It is clear that Jetton's joy is tied to her faith and both led her to her true love, as she shares that "I was trying to create something for myself before I came up with Abeela Sweets U Remember, then I woke up one morning and heard something say, 'I gave you hands, use them'." Knowing what the 'something' was, Jetton went into her kitchen and found that everything she needed for baking was already there. She began to bake and has been able make cakes and pies for hundreds of people, including seniors, patrons of cafes that serve her creations, churches, and others.

Jetton realized that a lot of people enjoy her cooking. "My long-term goal is to run my own cafe or a food truck but never in my wildest dreams did I think that I would be able to bake! and I mean I was so amazed. I did not know that I could bake the way that I bake."

Some things you learn and never lose. For Jetton, there are treasured lessons at the core of her kitchen skills. The first is cooking from scratch, meaning, she says, "it does not come out of a box. You're using every [real] ingredient that goes in whatever it is you're cooking and also measuring." And she might add, that leads to new creations, "I had extra things in my kitchen, and I said 'okay, well let me see what I can do'. After I began to make those and serve them to people for free and then people wanted to buy them, in the beginning I sold more of my sweet and salty nutty squares than my pastries. It's really quick and easy delicious treat and it's a fun thing for children's parties."

Jetton continues to enjoy creating those and other treats, which reveals her second prized joy – that she truly does start dishes and treats, alike, from scratch, "Even when I bake, I no longer use a measuring cup. In the beginning I used measure everything to the T and now like my grandmother, I can bake a cake and make anything without even measuring."

Where she formerly wondered how that kind of perfection was possible, Jetton is confident as she laughingly reports, "now I know, cuz after you do something so long it's just there. And you might add just a little bit more of this or of that and it just makes it extra good."

Cooking from scratch and without prescribed measuring adds to her kitchen credibility, but Jetton's joy flows from many sources which she describes as "just taking the time to put the love and the enjoyment of being in the kitchen knowing when I'm doing the product that I create that it's being given to someone for their family or for them to enjoy."

Like most cooks, Jetton cares deeply about how her food is presented and received by those who consume it. Her love is reflected in the shared joy between cook and consumers. She is open to criticism and suggestions, but rarely receives any. Instead, in a delicious circle of love, her motivation creates their delight, which refuels her joy. "I think what I enjoy most about cooking is watching people and hearing people say they enjoyed it or [hearing them] say, 'hmmm this is really good'. So I enjoy it… it gives me pleasure to watch others enjoy what my hands prepare."

As in any well-crafted art, the creator's joy is evident, engages all her senses, and overflows to others. "I don't know… just putting my all into creating… I like the sounds of the mixers going, okay? I really enjoy sound of the mixers", she laughs. "And the mixtures coming together. I just enjoy cooking. I like creating. I like coming up with new ideas and I just know that the possibilities of having what I desire is in this."

    Faith, joy, love. The main ingredients for Jetton Neal, a 54-year-old mother of three adult children and five grandchildren. One of her favorites that is a real crowd pleaser is her Sweet & Salty Nutty Squares. She hopes you'll try them.

SWEET & SALTY NUTTY SQUARES

Ingredients
- 1 10oz Bag Hershey Chocolate Chips
- 1 8oz Chopped Nuts (your choice)
- Sea Salt
- Cookie Sheet
- Glass Bowl
- Med Sauce Pan
- Wax Paper
- Chopping Board

Preparation
1. Add 2 cups of water to sauce pan over medium heat and bring to a boil.
2. Add glass bowl on top of saucepan and pour in the chocolate chips.
3. Stir until completely melted, remove glass bowl, add chopped nuts.
4. (chop nuts smaller is optional) stir until evenly mixed.
5. Put sheet of wax paper on cookie sheet, pour
6. mixture on wax paper and spread evenly. (not to thin)
7. After spreading to your likeness, take a pinch of sea salt and sprinkle over the top.
8. Put in the freezer for 10 min, then remove.
9. Peel from wax paper, add to chopping board and carefully cut into squares.

ENJOY!!!

Janice Hawthorne Griffin
Barbara Huddleston
Brenda Huddleston
LaShell Livingston McGee

SPIRITUAL MEDITATION:
A TALE OF QUILTING, FOUR COUSINS, AND A
FAMILY LEGACY

Chapter Five

Although Mrs. Lounell "Nell" Huddleston Hawthorne is deceased, her memory lives on in the quilting circle which bears her name and carries on a family legacy. Each of the four women in Nell's Quilting Circle are drawn to the art of quilting and to this particular circle of quilters for different, yet interwoven reasons.

We also honor the memory of the late Barbara Huddleston, interviewed for this story. She transitioned and became one of the ancestors in September 2023.

WE'VE GOT A STORY TO TELL: A STORY OF LOVE AND LEGACY

For Janice Hawthorne Griffin, it is a love affair with fabrics. She describes quilts and tells stories about them that evoke memories and images of love and warmth wrapped in the very fabric. There were "britches" quilts stitched together by her grandmother and aunts. Her relationship with fabrics is itself one that is woven together, consisting of childhood memories of being fascinated by bright colors, patterns, and interesting textures while learning to sew in a Girl Scout troop, and being taught more about sewing by her mother. Listening to Janice, it is easy to ascertain that as she was continuing to add to her skills when taking home economics in high school, she grew even fonder of bright colors and interesting patterns on a variety of textures. "It was always fascinating to me to go to Sears Roebuck & Company and go to the fabric department and buy a pattern…" she says, and figure out which fabric would be suitable.

Janice loves to touch the material in the fabric store, but her deep love springs more so from a fascination with the prints, imagining their transformation into what they can become. "So to me that was always the creative part, the reason I love fabric to this day." The love that sprouted when she first learned to sew as a Girl Scout continued to grow in adulthood, so much that at one point, she claims, "I probably had enough fabric in my house to open my own fabric store."

Her cousin, Barbara Huddleston, could relate to Janice's love of color. "I love color and I like to see how colors mixes and match so that they work together," Barbara says. Laughing, she also admits to being "a feeler," like her cousin. "I like to touch it and rub it and to like what I'm touching and feeling." As she does so, Barbara admits, she wonders about her ancestors, asking herself, "When they made quilts, the part that touched your body was always plain cotton, either they knew it or felt it… how it breathes because it's a living thing… cotton and wool are next to your body, were the natural fabrics… whatever was on the top. But it was always plain next to your skin".

Barbara pointedly acknowledged that many memories are, for her, fuzzy. She has a sharp recollection of being in the presence of quilters in action, with fabrics of varying hues and textures spread across quilting horses set up in her grandmother Sadie's home in East St. Louis which parallels that of the protective, comforting weight of the finished quilts that her other grandmother used to covered her in Forest City, Arkansas. As she settled in bed their weight and warmth snugly secured her in one spot, working far better than the popular modern-day "weighted blankets." Barbara's memories traverse time, space, and place through generations of women.

Another member of their circle is LaShell Livingston. LaShell is Barbara, Brenda, and Janice's cousin. She has deep southern roots. With parents from Macon, Georgia, unlike her cousins, LaShell grew up in a military family that moved around quite a bit. Quilting wasn't a part of her story, she says. She does not have early stories of a mother's and grandmother's influence on quilting. Instead, she shares her recollection of her teachers' efforts to shape student's aspirations according to the norms of the times. The least talkative of the four women, LaShell pointed out that she learned to sew because it was expected of the girls, whom teachers urged to look forward to futures as homemakers. She remembers how the Home Economics teachers "would put that paper on that sewing machine and we would have to stitch across that line, a technique unfamiliar to Janice and Barbara. Although she recognized and privately resented the societal assumption and limitations regarding her future, LaShell gleaned some benefit and now acknowledges the practicality in learning to quilt.

When she finally got to St. Louis "for the second time," LaShell was introduced to quilting because Janice's mother quilted. Prior to that, she says," I didn't even know about the quilting; it was just on the bed." She recalls beginning to work together with the women on projects, a new experience for her. In short time, LaShell was hooked and soon relished the relaxing chance to "sit around and talk and quilt and things like that," she said, adding "just to come to know about how to quilt for real because my family wasn't into all of that." LaShell listens intently when the other two women share family stories, occasionally adding her own, as when she jokingly tells of their husband's take on their gatherings to quilt. "We enjoyed doing it. But overhearing the laughter, whispers, and comments, the husbands… they say "Y'all been over there talkin' bout us,'" she said.

Cousin Brenda Huddleston joined in to tell a bit of her story. One of the first things she shares is about her faith. She says "I am a Christian, a wife, a mother, a grandmother, and an educator. I have been married for 38 years. [I] was educated through the St. Louis public school system; kindergarten through college. At that time Harris Teacher's College was a part of the public school system. After receiving my BA degree from Harris, I went on to receive an MA from the University of Missouri in St. Louis, and an administrative certification from Southern Illinois University in Edwardsville." Now, with all of that said, the joy in my life is my family and what we share, and quilting has been a big part.

I made my first quilt, by myself, for my doll. It was a blue and white nine-patch. And of course, I learned to do that by watching my grandmother and aunts quilt when I visited their house on the weekend.

This family's ancestral aesthetic speaks of a historical connection to quilting that authorities in the field sometimes overlook or underplay. But historians who recognize the connecting threads so clearly woven into the historical fabric of the lives and work of contemporary quilters point out the experiences of men and women transplanted from many regions of the African continent. It is a legacy that will continue through many more generations, embedded in the memories, and conveyed in the stories told to those who actively and passively listen. Grandmothers play a pivotal role in transmitting the stories. They are the muse, whose living actions carried the tradition and whose words rolled from their tongue as they threaded needles and herstory.

If you follow closely, you'll discover a familiar, yet fascinating story woven together through generations and across family lines. Mama Sadie, who was the grandmother, also influenced their love of quilts. Barbara says "I was at their house more often than my own mom's family because they are from Forest City, Arkansas,"

Brenda shared that the love of sewing and quilting "is in our blood" and comes from our great, great, great grandmother. Amanda Aydelotte. Brenda shared some of her history.

HISTORY OF THE AYDELOTTE FAMILY

Subsequent to Alberta's account which was recorded in 1976, the original history has been amended to reflect ongoing research and recollections by other family members. This history will continue to be amended and updated to reflect additional research.
Author – Alberta Jackson Barnett.

"Amanda Aydelotte was born in 1834 (approximate) in Virginia to a slave mother and white father who were also born in Virginia. She called herself Amanda Jay Gould or Amanda Lucy Melvinne Fitzsally Aydelotte[1]*. When asked why or how she got her name, said she didn't know, but that for some reason she liked it. She was affectionately known as "Gram" by her family.*

Amanda said when she found herself it was at the tender age of ten or less. Sometime during the early 1840's she and her mother were slave servants in a prominent home in Hopkinsville, Kentucky or maybe Hodgensville, KY. She remembered that on one occasion, the family she was a servant to, entertained a president of the United States, Zachary Taylor[2]. According to custom, she passed the cup with the golden chain to the company. She would often brag that she had served a president of the United States.

    Amanda and her mother were passed on to another slave-owner who was a doctor in St. Louis, Missouri. The doctor became very heavy in debt and had to sell them. Amanda recalled hearing her mother ask the doctor "Master Why?" and that he made it plain to her he had to because of his indebtedness. Amanda, her mother and reportedly an arm baby were put on a boat on the Mississippi River in St. Louis, Missouri and shipped down to Memphis, Tennessee. There, they were placed on an auction block and Amanda was sold for $1,000 to a slave-owner named Sugars McLemore[3] in approximately 1845. He had traveled from Brownsville, Tennessee on a log wagon. Amanda asked McLemore to buy her mother, he told her he brought only $1,000 with him and could not purchase her mother. Her mother was then placed on a boat and the last Amanda saw of her; she was headed on down the Mississippi River. This made her very unhappy and she remembers crying all the way to her new home in Brownsville. Finally, McLemore told her to stop crying, he would be good to her.

    Amanda finished growing up as a house servant in the home of Sugars McLemore until 1856. She was given to one of his daughters, Nancy "Nannie" Dabney McLemore[4] as a personal servant. Amanda came up weaving cloth and making dresses of fine laces and silks for her young mistress. When the mistress discarded the clothes, they became Amanda's. Amanda and another slave girl (personal servant to Nannie's sister) would ride in the surrey with their mistresses to attend the McLemore sisters, as was the custom of that day. Amanda and the other slave girl were of like situations, having been born of slave mothers and white fathers. There also was a male slave who drove the surrey. Amanda said it was talked among the people that the servant girls were prettier and looked better than their mistresses (especially wearing the fine clothes passed back to them).

Amanda's mistress married Thomas "Theo" Cole on May 10, 1856. On December 10, 1856 Frank Aydelotte was gifted by Sugars McLemore to his daughter Nannie McLemore Cole. Sugars McLemore stipulated in his deed that Frank would be owned solely by his daughter Nannie and her heirs.

Nannie moved from Brownsville, TN to Madison County, Tennessee. Amanda and her children went with her to Jackson, TN. Frank Aydelotte was a slave on Sugars McLemore's plantation. He had formerly come from Virginia to Frankfort, Kentucky, then to Madison County, Tennessee under different slave-owners. When the roll was called, he would wait until they called him "Frank Aydelotte". This is the first name he had been aware of and thus did not suffer another name change. Frank and Amanda were married in 1855. Their children called him Pap. Pap passed away in 1901 and was buried in the Epperson Cemetery. His tombstone bears the inscription "Asleep in Jesus". It stands strong today and mark his final resting place.

Amanda was the mother of seventeen children[5]. Jennie, Josie, Ida, Ellen, and Narcissis were born slaves[6]. Lula, Dinah and John Samuel 'aka Buddy' were born after emancipation, however they all were mulattos. Eliza and Dora were born free.

Gram was a very clever person coming up through slavery. She was gifted with many talents; she was great with the needle which was extended through her family. Many of her daughters could sew. She was a servant, not only to her master and mistress, but was a practical nurse, plus a midwife throughout the neighborhood of Black and white. With doctors and on her own, this too was learned by her children.

She was a soul that loved music. She could sing all the old spirituals of that day. She had a very high soprano voice that grew higher as the years passed. The grandchildren would often smile at some of her high notes. Her son Buddy bought her a zither[7] from an agent passing through the countryside. Amanda would pick out tunes she knew to sing, which afforded her much pleasure.

Her son Buddy, a very kind and loving person, kept a home for his mother. When necessary, his sisters, many nieces and nephews lived with he and Gram, many family members married out of that home.

Gram was confined to the bed for the last seven years of her life. Often her grandchildren would watch her while their parents were away. Amanda never lost her kind and lovable ways and was a nice person with a good disposition and liked by everyone that knew her. Amanda passed away in May of 1924, Madison County, Tennessee and was laid to rest in the Henry Cole Cemetery (old St. John Church Cemetery)."

NOTES:

[1] Some of her grandchildren were named Amanda, Lucy and Melvinne.

[2] Zachary Taylor lived from 1784-1850 and was the 12th President of the United States from 1849-1850. He lived in Lexington, KY which is near Hodgenville, KY. Historians in Hopkinsville, KY can find no record of Zachary Taylor ever visiting Hopkinsville.

[3] Sugars McLemore was born in 1795 in Franklin County, North Carolina. The McLemore family immigrated to the U.S. from Argyleshire, Scotland around 1720. After the treaty with the Indians of West Tennessee was signed (early 1820's) by Andrew Jackson, Sugars was sent to West Tennessee by the University of North Carolina to survey the land. He surveyed Haywood, Madison and Crockett counties and was given 1/6 of the land as compensation, thus making him a very large landowner. He settled in Brownsville, Tennessee, was married three times and died in 1867. He was buried on the family farm in Bells, Tennessee in the Bottom.

[4] Nancy Dabney McLemore Cole was Sugars McLemore eighth child. She was born in 1836.

[5] We could only account for eleven of her children. The other six (possibly born between 1847 and 1854) were either sold or stillborn.

[6] Amanda named seven of her children after McLemore family members. They were Dora, Lula, John Samuel "Buddy", Narcissis, Eliza, Nanny, and Jennie.

[7] Zither - stringed musical instrument similar to a guitar.

REFERENCES / SOURCES:

1. **Alberta Jackson Barnett**, of Cincinnati, OH and one of Amanda's granddaughters provided the original historical account in 1976 for the first reunion.
2. **United States Federal Census:**

   1820 - Jefferson County, Kentucky   1860 – Hickman County, Kentucky

   1820 - Williamson County, Tennessee   1860 – Madison County, Tennessee

   1830 - Gibson County, Tennessee   1880 – Madison County, Tennessee

   1830 - Madison County, Tennessee   1900, 1910, 1920 – Madison County, Tennessee

   1830, 1840 and 1850 - Haywood County, Tennessee
3. **McLemore Family Research Files**

   Jackson/Madison County Library - Jackson, Tennessee
4. **Civil War Journal** of Rebecca McLemore Welborn, 1864
5. **1877 Land Ownership Record**, Madison County, Tennessee, District #9.
6. **The McLemore Search**, Fairy Bell McLemore Edwards - Canyon Lake, Texas
7. **Personal Recollections:** Some of Amanda's Grandchildren and Great-Grandchildren (notably, Ora Cole McLemore, Iona Huddleston Cole and Hayward Hobson).
8. **Deed of Gift, Sugars McLemore to Nannie McLemore Cole**. December, 1856 Deed Book, Jackson, TN, Jackson Madison Library.

Brenda Huddleston shared that her ancestor, Amanda, was the person who ushered in the family's love for sewing and quilting. "One of her tasks during enslavement was the creation of dresses for her mistress." Brenda carries on that tradition in her quilting. There's a photo of great, great, great grandmother Amanda on a beautiful quilt Brenda created. The quilt captures the family history, including the fact that her great, great, great grandmother Amanda was auctioned at the Old Courthouse in downtown St. Louis. "She was put on a boat and sent down the river to Memphis, Tennessee, where she was purchased by Sugars McLemore, a slave owner, in approximately 1845. In Memphis, Amanda was separated from her mother."

A SEED WAS PLANTED

The creative act of personal expression did much more than nurture four women. It germinated into a profound appreciation of beautiful fabric, the colors, and the possibilities they reflected. Much more than form, the pieces also offered literal and figurative functionality. "Those quilts did that at both my grandmother's houses…they just held you down,"

These quilter's mutual fondness shows through in the ease of their camaraderie – a conversation that flows like a summer's breeze, resonant with laughter and diffusing light around the room, as each woman instinctively comprehends the deeper meaning of this expressive form that they have so dearly embraced. The women credit Barbara with organizing their small "quilting bee." They got together in 2010 or 2011 at the urging of Janice's mother, who suggested that the group could teach the young girls in the family about quilting – which they did. Janice recalls being excited to see that we were able to get some of the children involved. The seed planted by the elder, watered by the next generation blossomed into an experience of new family traditions, closer relationships, and lots of discovery as they shared life's ordinary slices and special moments.

They are the carriers of the legacy left by Janice's mother Nell, now deceased, one firmly planted in their minds that often surfaces when Barbara reminisces about her "…She was a quilter from her heart. Brilliant! When you see her quilts, you'll agree with that." Barbara counts the nearly five years spent with her each week, "was a precious time for me to learn how to quilt … that was absolutely wonderful. She gave me a lot of good information about quilting and life during that time."

Through life's transitions, the women pass the valuable life and quilting skills to others. As Mother Nell did when she visited the neighborhood school her children attended, Barbara is particularly interested in teaching the youth, believing that "They need something to slow their brains down now because the world is giving them everything so fast and loud and hard and they have their headphones on and that noisy music is beating right into their brain." With the permanence of her grandmothers' and mother's lessons firmly imprinted in her heart, Janice notices the varying forms of expression of emotions and the creativity that emerge. "One thing I have noticed, some family members have kept it very simple,' including the original members. "I have noticed that LaShell has an eye for catching the unusual, putting together patterns that you wouldn't think would go together. That's one of her gifts." Among others, it is clear, that LaShell appreciates her role in this family legacy and graciously shares what she brings.

The profound impact that Brenda, Janice, LaShell, and Barbara have shared with other family members from their own skills and Mother Nell's wealth of knowledge travels along the ancestral paths of the grandmothers, great-grandmother, great-great grandmothers, all the way back to great-great-great grandmother Amanda that came before. Janice makes clear the importance of what is transmitted to younger ones and points out that "it's more than just the skill I think. I can remember as a child you hear so many life lessons from older people talking; in memory of my Mom we always get together right after Christmas and New Year. We call it the Nell's Memorial Quilting/Christmas Bee… like I say it's more than just skill… it's also to teach them and even pass down a lot of the traditions that we have been taught."

The women's respect for their history, future, and each other resonates in their interaction and art. In Janice's contemplative preferences, inform her choices of older fabrics. In Barbara's assessment of quilting as "spiritual meditation and fellowship." And Janice's affirmation that "when we are at our quilting bees, it can be spiritual." The women agree that because of the necessary work of women who came before, they understand and are now able to enjoy the craft. As Janice says, "Sometimes when I'm stitching, I'm thinking that our ancestors are smiling so it's a way for me to feel connected to the ancestors and to let them know that their skills and craft did not fall by the wayside."

Amanda "Gram" Aydelotte and some of her family on a Sunday afternoon following worship service. This picture was possibly made in 1911.

1st Row, L-R: *Amanda "Gram" Aydelotte, Mona Lenton, Frank "Bub" Huddleston, Iona Huddleston, Walsh Huddleston, Zollner Lenton, Fate Huddleston*
2nd Row, L-R: *Eliza Aydelotte Dotson Cole, Sophia Huddleston, Alexander "Preacher" Dotson, Lula Aydelotte Huddleston, (Lula is holding her grandson, Booker T. James), Sadie Huddleston, Canary Huddleston, Carlos Huddlestor*
3rd Row, L-R: *Herman "Hutt" Huddleston, John James, Silena Dotson, Everett Huddleston, Alma Huddleston*

Carlos and Sadie Huddleston, and youngest child Shari

Carlos and Sadie Huddleston, and youngest child Shari

Sadie Huddleston and her three children; Samuel Huddleston (L), Lounell Huddleston-Hawthorne (C), and Hoyie Huddleston (R).

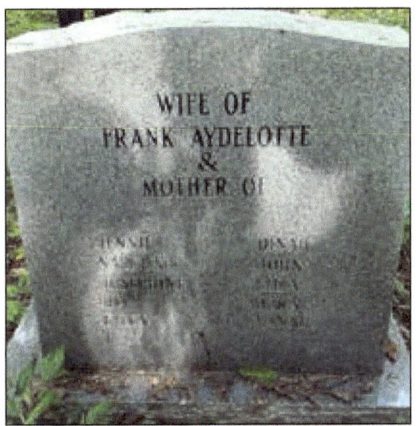

Brenda Huddleston, Monica Huddleston, Cameron Hubbard, Tjuana Huddleston

Samuel Wynn

Brenda Huddleston

Monica Huddleston, Mya Huddleston, Cheryl Huddleston, Ida Mae Huddleston, Tjuana Huddleston, Janice Hawthorne Griffin

LaShell Livington, Janice Hawthorne Griffin, Olivia Huddleston-Boatman, Troy White, Tjuana Huddleston

Oliver Huddleston-Boatman, Tjuana Huddleston, Janice Hawthorne Griffin, Barbara Huddleston, Brenda Huddleston, Detria Huddleston, Cameron Hubbard, Monica Huddleston

Gloria Arrington and Frances Jones

Pamela Coaxum

OF FASCINATION, FABRICS, AND FAMILY

Chapter Six

> *"The spirits of my family come through when I'm doing the sewing and the quilting..."* ~Pamela Tucker Coaxum

> *"...the ancestors are delighted"* ~Aunt Ionis

Quilting conjures up memories and a myriad of ideas in the mind of the quilter. For Pamela Tucker Coaxum it is the spirit of family. Pamela's creativity connects her to her family's belief in the power of Proximity, Ancestral Legacy, Education, and stories. Taken together, she believes one can accomplish many things. Touching fabric and simultaneously touching the lives of others is an inextricable experience drawing her close to her matrilineal legacy of Creativity. Pamela's high school sewing lessons offered a seamless path to the exploration of quilting in later life. A path that weaves together the spirit of family strength, resilience, and achievement from the fabrics of their lives. Pamela's rich family history includes generations of women who are teachers and extraordinarily creative artists that have sewn and quilted for generations.

   A former corporate executive and community nonprofit facilitator. Pamela understands the importance of the threads that comprise the contours of the family's heritage. Her heritage highlights tell of a deep reverence for teaching family and others, self-expression and preservation of family unity and community. Pamela shares bits of her own story, one of migration that joined her mother from the small Tennessee town of Tiptonville with her father from East St. Louis, Illinois and taking them to the city of Minneapolis, Minnesota. This migration carries a fascinating connection to her life. "I'm a 5th [generation] family. My parents migrated to Minnesota, but the important thing is that they were visual artists, and my mom has a real famous picture with my mother and Georgia O'Keefe at FISK University, so I just say everything is in my family. My other aunt taught the Florida highwaymen and the last remaining sister is in Connecticut and she does exhibits and things, so it's kind of an art form in our family… it's been for generations so when my great aunt passed, I have some of her quilts that were handmade probably in the 40s. But I have been sewing for a long time, and I've been quilting since 2005."

Pamela's community commitment connected her full circle, placing her squarely in the family legacy. "We did a camp at my church and this lady who quilts said "let's make a quilt." And that's how I got into quilting… since 2005. My mother was a sewer, my grandmother was a sewer, and her sisters were sewers and my mother and all of them are artists." The proof is in the fabric. Exploring the fabric's connection to the women who taught her to quilt, Pamela recalls "we would go to Chicago in the summer and I used to love going to my grandmother's basement and she had stacks and stacks of fabric. Just stacks of fabric and that's what I have! I've got it in tubs now."

Pamela allows the fabric to lead her along the river of ancestral memory, and delight when that journey connects her to Africa. "We did an African ABC quilt, and finding the right kind of fabric for African themes was really hard, you know, like a hut… what kind of fabric do you use for a hut? Or what kind of fabric do you use for a monkey? Or what kind of fabric do you use for a rhinoceros to really show their texture and depth of their patterns?" In similar fashion, when working with a group of children in East St. Louis, Pamela prompts them to let the fabric feed their imaginations as they choose the right colors and textures to tell stories.

She carries in her own spirit the legacy of giving that lies at the core of some artist's creativity. She conveys a love of her pieces rooted in an appreciation of both form and function. She explains that "there is nothing like the sense of accomplishment and then it's the gift… I remember when I first started quilting a friend of mine said, 'now don't you start giving all your quilts away' but that's exactly what I've done. Every time I make them, somebody else has them or a family member says, 'can I have this?' and I say 'yes!', I'm quick to put my label on it. But it's that sense of accomplishment, like any artist it goes to certain people, you have to know they appreciate your art form and time. You know some people may want a quilt, but you don't know if you want to give it to them because you don't know if they'll appreciate it. So, I think there is a whole complexity of all of that."

In 2005, Pamela was urged by a member to do a quilt with children in the church summer camp. Following that, she began her quilting journey. It started with a t-shirt quilt Pamela made as a graduation gift for her son, chronicling his outstanding football career as one of the top players in the St. Louis region. Since then Pamela recounts that T-shirt quilt was followed by "probably about seven of them done for friends." Pamela was so fascinated by the T-shirts they pick and the story they tell," that she is now considering creating her own T-shirt quilt.

With 15 years of experience, Pamela may consider herself a relatively new quilter, but she has no plans to stop anytime soon. And in the years to come, her plans include pushing the boundaries of creativity, exploring history, passing down the spirit of family artistry, and fulfilling her dreams of doing a lot more work with applique. She sees expansive possibilities in the works displayed at quilt shows, such as that of an African American woman whose family reunion quilt wowed Pamela and won best of show at the American Quilting Society in Paducah, Kentucky a couple of years ago. Awed and impressed by the quilter's skill, artistry and stitched story of her family's journey from slavery through current times, Pamela vowed to expand her own initial foray into designing a family quilt.

Having created a quilt years ago which she recalls as "probably my second one, so my corners didn't always meet and such but there are pictures of my family in it…" Pamela says she wants to do more with quilting and reveals that at night, when she thinks about the quilts she could make, she envisions an applique creation that brings to vivid life the story of her own family, or another creation that reflects nature's beauty, "not necessarily the forest kind of vision…I like flowers, grass and butterflies. There's something about sewing and fabric and putting that together and making it look real and giving it that life that appeals to me." Pamela's quilting dreams stretch out before her, covering the years ahead with idea after idea. "One of the things I've wanted to do in the back of my mind is a pictorial of quilting along the Mississippi, and the reason why I thought of that is because, you know, closer to slavery days, African American communities were in the wetlands along the Mississippi and that's kind of how my family migration pattern is from Tiptonville, Tennessee along the Mississippi up to St. Louis – my dad was from East St. Louis... up through Minneapolis, which is where I was born. And to try to find African American historical quilters along the Mississippi would be a fascinating story."

Part teacher, part artist, part historian, Pamela has already left an indelible mark on children in St. Louis County and East St. Louis through her nonprofit community work, beginning with participants in the Camp Angel run by her church, serving children in foster care. Over time, she has introduced children in East St. Louis to quilting, proving to naysayers that children's imaginations and attention could be captured by the creative, hands-on nature of the project. While others doubted that children with trauma-related emotional, social, or behavioral disorders would respond positively, Pamela considerately but confidently forged ahead. Her idea worked, and recalling the camp's success she effuses, "but I'll tell you they loved that quilting so much that next year they remembered our names! And it was therapeutic... it's the touching... you know how close you have to get to the children when you are doing their hands... and we did two hand quilts, and this year we did a heart quilt... and it has just been fabulous! Her goal now is "to introduce a quilt into every agency in East St. Louis."

Harriet Mucherson

WOW, SHE MAKES GOOD CAKES!

Chapter Seven

Traditions don't happen in a day, and usually, neither does delicious food. Harriet Mucherson is proof positive that this is truth. Her story is one in which any child would play the lead role. Imagine a home filled with love and warmth. A mother whose command of the kitchen was well known and welcomed by all around. Being a child whose love of being in that space, watching, learning – and taste-testing – was one of life's great joys.

"As a kid I was always in the kitchen with my mom. We would have a tradition of, like at Halloween for instance, coming up…so for then, chili was our tradition. She would do chili, and cupcakes, and we would have a Halloween party with some of the kids in the neighborhood." Harriet describes the same atmosphere of celebration being created for Christmas when the established tradition was baking. Her memories of food and family continue to feed Harriet's love of cooking, and especially baking. Memories of her Aunt Lucille, a "wonderful cook" and her daughter, "who makes the best zucchini bread and she's like 96 years old right now," Harriet notes with respectful awe. "I want to have a zoom call with her so that I can get that recipe." It's no wonder that good food and the fellowship it would bring was commonplace in the Mucherson household. The picture becomes clearer and more interesting as she adds, "My dad's sisters were amazing cooks too. So I've always been a bit of a foodie." Throw in a cousin or two, like Mike, who traveled the world and shared his experiences with Harriet, and "turned me onto a lot of different foods," and you have the makings of a perennial, self-described foodie with an admittedly "very eclectic palate."

Over the years, Harriet honed an "at least try it once" philosophy, reasoning that one can always make an informed decision to refuse an unappealing dish on a subsequent occasion. That openness to trying a variety of foods has led to an accumulation of some recipes, a number of them locked in her memory, and others she hopes to solicit from older relatives and even cousins in her peer group. And of course, there are mom's recipes – those her mother received, recorded, and recreated for her own family just as Harriet's grandmother had also done. Recipes that tell the story of Harriet's mother's heritage, but also the legacy left for those who would carry on the flavors, aromas, and traditions. Mucherson's own creations mixed with favorites adapted from family and friends, specialties borrowed from church and club members – all written down and tucked away. Altogether, these recipes are a treasure waiting to be rediscovered, and Harriet vows to successfully unearth and give her mother's collection of edible bliss new life. "My mom," she begins, "actually… I was trying to find her cookbook and I packed it away and I gotta go dig for it." The collection of recipes from church ladies and club sisters, in-laws and neighbors nestled with those handed down through the years are hidden among Harriet's possessions. "I just have to locate it but some of the recipes I kind of just remember."

As her voice trails off, it's clear that Harriet's thoughts have traveled to time and place about which she might willingly share if prompted.

"It was always warm. It was always warm. Just the smells that would trigger… like pies cooking and then that triggered that flavor so then I'd go and start looking it up and trying to cook that and if she baked rolls or just homemade rolls. So I tried that and I did my first rolls. My mom would do them all the time but I did my first rolls maybe a year ago I guess and I gave them to Tracy and my guy's sister and they gave them a thumbs up. I was happy with the turnout."

Harriet loves to cook, but lights up when she clarifies, "I just like to bake! I like to experiment with different foods, but baking, I enjoy that. Pies I can do but I still have to master that craft because the crust has to be just right, temperature has to be just so before you can… because I've thrown a lot of things down the drain and in the trash just trying to experiment and trying to get it just right."

"You know old cooks back in the day really didn't measure and I would ask my aunts and my mom… so how much do you put in there? And they said just a handful or a pinch. So I'd say what is a handful… my hand? Because I got a big hand. So is it my hand… or is it a pinch or a handful in your hand? So what exactly is that? But when you're baking, they have to be pretty precise. Your liquid measure has to be in a liquid measuring cup and the dry measure has to be for the dry ingredients. Things have to be at the right temp and so I do. I lay out everything according to whatever recipe that I am going to tackle and just start incorporating it. Sometimes after I make something I will do a twist and add something else just to see how that turns out."

While Harriet is in the kitchen baking, her process engages all of her senses, and is the start of her connection to what she is preparing and to those who will consume the final dish. "How is the person going to respond? How will they respond to the 'something special' that I did in creating the item?" That's very important to me and hopefully they like it and if they don't, I like feedback because I think feedback is very important. I know everybody's tastes are different but the presentation for me is important as well."

"I have pictures and even when I'm putting them into the box that I'm giving, I like to put little inspirational messages on the box and feel good positive things on there too. But that's all into the presentation because the presentation is 98% and taste is maybe 100% because that's with anything. The presentation is key. And I do it with, you know, a positive heart and love behind it."

"You have to experiment and because we all have life changes with our health and still want to be able to enjoy it, and you can always cultivate a taste or pretty much anything... at least my taste buds can. Because I don't really like sweet tea, I can drink it plain. Soda I cut out 15 or so years ago, but it's the effervescence of the soda that I like so I drink seltzer and now they have exploded the market with flavored seltzer. Just trying to make different changes and you can enjoy everything, just within moderation, which is just hard."

Her story may have similarities to the legends we read or hear about, those who become successful restaurateurs. But despite the love of sharing her culinary creations with others – especially by baking – Harriet's passion is fulfilled as she prepares meals for family and friends, and she has no desire to own a restaurant.

Fearing that the magic may become lost, Harriet is clear that her endeavor is for enjoyment and fun. "If I happen to make something monetarily out of it, that's fine but not really. Tracy, a cousin, keeps pushing me toward that end goal because I did a couple meal preps for her mom." Harriet notes, "that's the difference – having to and wanting to. I do enjoy it. I can do it every day," she says with a hint of glee in her voice and twinkle in her eyes. "I'm getting ready to do the chili and everything for Halloween. My God sisters will come over and, you know, we'll have that and continue that tradition, as well. She asks, " Are you cooking anything anytime soon?"

It makes sense that the upcoming observance of Halloween would involve food. The tradition in her family reflects not only the love of food, but of its meaning and ability to strengthen or cement connections with loved ones and strangers, as well. So focusing on the fun of the day, there are cupcakes or a cake and making sure the children and young people enjoy the decorations that reference autumn and the element of spookiness.

If anything confirms Harriet's love of gathering family and friends with good food, it's the holidays. Even as she recognizes the lingering impact of the COVID pandemic, this dedicated keeper of family traditions is encouraged that some restrictions have been modified or lifted. Things may be getting better, but Harriet is clear that "it is going to be different." Still, Thanksgiving remains her favorite holiday because, as Harriet explains, she always enjoyed the cooking part of it, adding enticing highlights of the gathering's usual menu of fried turkey and all the fixings. As she shares the joy of Thanksgiving's past, the committed cook acknowledges that she will "scale it down a lot this year because everybody's inside and not

With expectations for a limited Thanksgiving, Harriet envisions a better Christmas celebration; to avoid duplication of the Thanksgiving meal, the family feasts on lasagna, chicken wings, garlic bread, and a nice salad. A boost to the family tradition is that at least one person from the younger generations has caught the love of cooking. And it has added a little friendly competition to the Christmas meal. Harriet loves a dish created by her godson so much that Harriet's Christmas includes two versions of lasagna– his, with a white sauce, which she has deemed "Best of Show," and one of hers with a red sauce, which she insists is "the runner up." It's all in good fun, and the humor was not lost on the others when Harriet revealed that her choice of award is derived from the honors conferred in the highly regarded AKC National Dog Show. Harriet insists that the white sauce dish is really good and agrees that hers - a spinach version, is a very close runner-up, the vegetable one, that's good.

The fun of Harriet's ranking is not lost on her loved ones because even though they know the source of the title bestowed on the younger cook, they also know her sentiment about his food is from the heart. Harriet explains that during the Christmas season, the AKC National Dog Show would air on television, and it struck her that the 'Best of Show' was such a coveted honor. She chuckles, concluding her story with a sincere compliment and an expert's respect for another's skill, "It was so good and everything, so he was always Best in Show. It really is so good. He gave me the recipe for that once. I said mine is good, but his is Best in Show."

Her godson's interest in cooking pleases Harriet, but she laments that other than that, her cousin Tracy is the only one who will cook. "She doesn't bake really but she'll cook," Harriet says. This makes mentoring others in the family difficult because as she points out, "Nobody likes to COOK!" Smiling, she adds, "they like to eat. Yes, the other friends or relatives, they pretty much just eat. They don't cook. A lot of people don't like the process because it is time consuming, but I like that part. That doesn't bother me. That's part of the joy of it, getting to the end result that I like. My son will cook… he hasn't baked a lot, but he does amazing wings and other dishes."

For those who will continue the family traditions by cooking, passing along recipes and ideas, as well as those who will continue to enjoy the food, fellowship, and fun, passing on the tradition of participation, Harriet hopes that they will always appreciate and share the deeper meaning of food – not just eating, but what says about them – who they are as individuals that are part of immediate and extended families and communities uniquely and positively shaped by its purpose and power.

The value that food holds for Harriet is rooted in love and the laughter, togetherness, stories, and memories that food holds; the recipes and traditions she learned were quite simply, vital pieces of the relationships formed and developed over time. Accompanied by invaluable lessons about life and love, Harriet's relationship with food offers a healthy appreciation of its purpose and also its power. Her conversation references pleasure and simultaneously recommends balance and expresses a reverent respect that all this is transmitted as it naturally nurtures our beings. But beyond eating to live, this consummate cook stirs up more than dishes and delectables; her food fosters fellowship, reunion, and relationship among friends, family, and strangers, alike. She likens it to art, saying, "I think it brings us closer together. It's something you can share with your loved ones and with anybody. Sharing a meal with someone, that's important.

To share a meal with someone or to offer food can open up conversation. Just like if you went to an art gallery and shared a conversation about a piece. Just seeing people enjoy what you have done… It gives you a happy feeling. And when you do it out of love it's not just to nourish your tummy when you're hungry, it's nourishing your spirit, it nourishes your soul, I think that it's just community. It's community. And it is a service. When I cook I'm careful and I take as much care with what I'm doing for others as I would give to myself and my family."

Sprinkled with genuine care, and measured with love, Harriet prepares food to share, and will feed anyone; her meals extend beyond family and friends, to hungry neighbors, and others. Whatever she cooks or bakes is offered with the same degree of care to all in homage to her personal adage that says it all. "Everybody's gotta eat", she says, repeating with conviction...

"Everybody's Gotta Eat."

Sheryl Simmons

FOOD... IT'S A FAMILY THING

Chapter Eight

Sherly's love of cooking began in high school around freshman or sophomore year Her mother had 3 daughters, and she wanted them to have a meal prepared when she came home from work, so they took turns. It started with her oldest sister telling her "come on here to the kitchen, lemme show you how to do this." "So, while the sisters weren't quite as good as their mama, we could throw some things together before everybody got home."

The first thing she learned to cook was cornbread. Knowing the ingredients to put in, the meal vs the flour, the baking powder, a pinch of salt, eggs, and milk, well buttered milk at that time. She learned to use what we would call old school measurements. A pinch of this, a heaping teaspoon of that. "But believe me, you had to get it right. Because you were baking, some people think that if you don't use precise measurements then you can't bake, but that's just not true." Sheryl knows that with old school, they didn't really have precise measurements with tools. You have to be able to calculate visually, and have a good sense of taste and smell.

"After I took home economics class, I think junior year in high school, then they taught measurements and stuff and I learned a little more about that. But at home, my mom was old school."

Cooking was a social activity. "We talked and talked about, you know, about the day, of what was going on with different family members, and stuff like that." She describes it as like kind of like a girls' day out, but at home. She reminisced that everybody pitched in, sometimes all three of them would be in the kitchen. One of them would be washing the dishes, another one doing another chore, while the other did something else. "But we were all sisters, in there together." In that space, Sheryl felt love and just a sense of wellbeing. There was a sense of wholeness being in the kitchen with family and exchanging recipes, and "even now, good feelings come from those memories. So I think I enjoy cooking because it takes me back there a lot." Cooking was a form of celebration and showing love.

Sheryl says a lot of that understanding of intentionally showing love has been lost, especially in our African American community. "… a lot of ways that we show love came from that whole thing around the kitchen table, and mama's table, daddy's table, whoever was cooking at the time but at home and with love." She remembers watching the episode of Blackish and they were talking about fixing somebody's plate, and how women shouldn't be subservient "fixin" no man's plate, and he can fix his own plate. Then Marla Gibbs, who portrayed an elder family member explained that when she did it, it wasn't about all of those things, it was because the Black man has such a hard time out there in the world, and the world hated him and treated him not even like a man. So, the least she could do, when he got home, was to fix him something to eat so he would notice somebody loved him. Sheryl said that really resonated with her.

Sheryl had continued her traditions of celebration and acts of love, when she moved to St. Louis more than 35 years ago. She had a couple cousins in the city who were much older than her on her mother's side of the family. "They had a tradition where every holiday, one sister would take a holiday and we would cook… one person would cook the main dishes and the other people could bring like dessert or something to drink, but that person would maybe have the turkey or the ham or whatever." They would always celebrate around the table and laugh and talk creating those warm memories as well.

In her own household, she uses food pretty much the same way. "A lot of times I like to gather family and friends close around at the table and bring good cheer, especially in these times when so much is going on in the world… we still gather." She says they even did it during the COVID-19 pandemic. Sheryl is glad the worst of the pandemic is over. She now visits friends and family members, and participates in big celebrations, which she loves.

Her immediate family is much smaller, and the gatherings are much smaller but she still gathers people. She still cherishes the importance of providing them with good nourishment for the body, and the soul… as they gather together. "I think that's my way of showing love to them."

She also shows that same love by baking for someone, or carrying food to people who are shut-in and can't get out. It's a family thing. It's a cultural thing... It's a love thing.

Sheryl also talked about a connection to her earlier years of cooking in the kitchen with her sisters. "Well... I kind of like being in the kitchen by myself, but I do consider my daughters to be my sous chefs sometimes so that's a good thing, because that brings me back to when I was growing up." She says her husband cooks as well sometimes. "He barbeques really well. So if he's barbecuing she will let him do the barbecue and I will do something else so we kind of buddy up a little. It's really fun and creates more good memories."

She's always loved cooking, reading recipes and that kind of stuff. "... that has always been kind of a thing of mine, and I never really considered myself or wanted to be a chef until I got older, but I always like to look at pictures of food and collect recipes" so a lot of it to me is that you eat with your eyes first. So if it looks enticing you're going to want to taste it. But it's going to make you want it that much more."

Because Sheryl had an eye for beauty in her cooking, it probably inspired those around her. She noticed her youngest daughter was really big into pastries. "She's really big into baking, and we watched a lot of cooking shows together... and a lot of them always talked about presentation." Sheryl feels that presentation is everything. How does your plate look? So she became even a little bit more particular about that as she got older. "I think that it's important that you eat with your eyes first."

Nowadays, her favorite foods she likes to prepare are different types of chili, soups, and stews, especially in the fall and winter seasons. She says it reminds her of home and comfort. In addition to these heartwarming delights, her favorite is making her mother's cornbread dressing that she is sharing in this chapter.

MAMA'S CORNBREAD DRESSING

Ingredients

    1 ½ pans of cornbread

    2 – 4 slices of day old bread

    1 egg

    1 ½ Tbsp. dried sage

    (you can also add cooked giblets, sausage, or oysters if you choose)

    ¼ cup chopped celery

    ¼ cup chopped bell pepper

    ¼ cup chopped onion

    2 cups or more of pan drippings from your poultry (turkey, duck or chicken)

    1Tbsp. yellow mustard

    ½ Tsp. poultry seasoning

    1 stick melted butter

Preparation
1. Preheat oven to 350.
2. Grease oven safe baking dish.
3. Break up cornbread in a large bowl, add other ingredients, and mix thoroughly.
4. Pour dressing into greased dish and bake uncovered for 40 to 45minutes. Tester
5. should come out clean.
6. Remove from the oven and let sit for several minutes. Serve warm.

Edna Patterson Petty

CONSISTENCY AND CLARITY

Chapter Nine

> ***"Trust your instincts, trust your gut, and let your own light be your guide."*** ~ Edna Patterson Petty

For Edna Patterson Petty, clarity is important. Clarity about who you are. What you're doing. And what you're conveying, from the inside out. For instance, she makes it clear that she is from East St. Louis, Illinois. She is a fabric artist. And an art therapist. And without telling you, it quickly becomes clear that she is also passionate, compassionate, an amazing artist, astute therapist and community treasure.

Since she can remember, Edna has loved fabrics. Her mother made bed quilts from the family's old clothes and other fabrics. Snuggled beneath their warmth, nighttime became cozy walks down memory lane. Edna recalls, "When it was cold, you would be sitting out late nights wrapped in a quilt and you say 'this is from my skirt' or 'this is from my blouse' or something like that." Helping her mother "dismantle" the clothes as a child, Patterson remembers removing the waist from a skirt, taking off buttons and zippers, and "I was helping cut the fabric into sections", a process which captured her senses – touching different textures, the colors and feel of the fabrics being emblazoned in her young mind. "So I always had a passion for fabric," she muses, "always." By the time she was 15, Edna learned how to sew and began making her own clothes.

As a fabric artist, Edna says she doesn't buy new fabric, but taking a page from her childhood experience, reuses old clothing, some of which she finds at thrift stores. "I like doing recycling, and I got that from my mom…I don't buy new fabric…I reuse old clothing," she says, describing a process of visiting thrift stores to find pieces, and also accepting donated new fabric, using as many pieces and shapes of both to create recycled and repurposed art. This aspect of her artistry is gratifying to Edna, particularly in her work as an art therapist and especially with children. Her interest in conserving resources is transmitted organically by example in the process of her work with others. For instance, avoiding waste and simultaneously capturing more artistic shapes and cuts. Her tip that makes all the difference? "It's simply a matter of perception and practice. You just have to teach them how to look at things differently than they are looking at it," Edna offers.

Engaging in art and therapy with equal passion and proficiency allows Edna both joy and satisfaction. A natural teacher, from life's material and personal fragments, she draws meaning that infuses her personal work with life-altering wisdom through whose lessons she inspires the same in therapy clients.

In flowing words pieced together by swatches of memories, Edna weaves an oral, aural, visual narrative of what she learned from her mother translated into "what we were doing with the fabric…it was reconstructing… well deconstructing in one area because it was old skirts, old pants, old stories…so you took it down to just the scraps of fabric and then when it was reconstructed it was made into a bed quilt… so it was no longer a skirt or blouse… it was the sections of it," she offers. To that, she adds "so with the therapy part, you are working with feelings and with fabric. Well fabric and you're reconstructing that way so that's how I would put the two together whenever I was working with a group." Stitching it all together, Edna sums up what so many quilters have expressed, "whenever a person felt bad about themselves or no self-esteem whatsoever I had them create something on a small scale with fabric or whatever…something they could complete within that short time, trying to establish them completing something so they can feel good about themselves. You don't wanna give them something that's so hard that they can't finish it because then they're frustrated. But you give them something workable and then you build on that."

A consummate artist, Edna is clear about the artistry of quilting and her connection to it. In fact, her clarity in defining that relationship is in part a nod to the sanctity of the field. She notes that "The American Quilting Association defines a quilt as 3 layers: a top, a bottom, and a middle… which is the… batting…" and acknowledges that "whether I'm a fabric artist or whatever I would call myself, that's what connects it to the quilt is those 3 pieces of fabric, you know." When it comes to definitions, Edna's work definitely follows the path of the artist. It comes through in the work. "I might have a general idea of what I want it to look like, but once it starts working, it has a life of its own. I don't have any set way to get from Point A to Point B. And my design lets me know if it wants to stay the same size or grow".

The spirit of freedom in her artistry reflects a combination of Edna's innate creativity, her mother's influence and an insistence on authenticity that flows from within. She explains it as an inner voice; "Because you know you can have a piece that's too small… it looks stunted like it wants to spread its wings… so I listen to myself, my intuition, and gut reaction." That voice informs her work with others, as well, easing artistic tension and sensing the creative connection that infuses great art. "It's good for people to know about each other when they are working together on something, each 'knowing who they are' and contributing what they value to the project." Working alone or with others, this authenticity reflects the personal and artistic clarity that speaks through her work with fabric and offers valuable wisdom to people.

*"**Be individual, be you, go in the direction that you want to go.**"*

Patricia "Tish" Carroll

THE CHICKEN SOUP LADY

Chapter Ten

Now what would a cookbook be without a good chicken soup recipe? Well, if the reviews and recommendations of those who have been nourished and healed by Patricia Carroll's (Tish) recipe are any indication, this one won't let you down. Considering that adjectives like 'fantastic,' 'healing,' 'delicious,' 'soul warming,' were expressed more than once we had to taste for ourselves. Our own taste test coupled with phrases 'like mama made,' 'better than my mother's.' (yes, someone dared), and 'should be marketed and sold in stores', revealed we agreed with the original high praise. The story of the savory broth's inclusion here is but a confirmation of its legendary reputation.

True to her nature, Tish takes it all in stride. You'd never know that she considers her soup as good as others proclaim. The only hint is the way that out of genuine concern and generosity, she selflessly offers to whip up a pot when someone is 'under the weather.'

For years, Tish was the only girl in the family. She had four brothers, and their mother taught all of them to cook. Tish admits that she didn't really want to learn how to cook when her mother was trying to teach her. She recounts, "I was the only girl with four brothers for 14 years before my little sister was born. You know I just really wasn't into it, so I would burn the meal. She caught on to what I was doing and told me if I burned any more food, I was gonna be in trouble. So I stopped that." Still, she had picked up early on how to cook from her mother. Like many women, Tish's story is proof-positive of how much is learned and retained when one shadows a seasoned cook in the kitchen. "I was probably 10ish when I started really helping her in the kitchen. We had a gas stove, and they really didn't want me at the stove. I guess before then when I was 6 or 7, she would let me stir whatever she was making, like the cake batter." And besides, time spent eating the batter or whatever other tasty prep items are in the making also helps hone a fine-tuned palate. "So I don't consider that to be the cooking, but I was seeing what she was doing." With a mother who did not cook from recipes, Tish learned that the dash of this and a pinch of that, a smidgeon here and a taste along the way were the measurements and final surety that a dish was well-prepared.

Now, back to the soup with roots deeply embedded in Tish's sensory perceptions. She describes an "open" kitchen as she was growing up from which the family could smell the food cooking. From her years at home with the family Tish remembers taking in the characteristics of the food from beginning to end. Her mother prepared a variety of meals, she says, and for each "you knew how it smelled, what it looked like when it was done, and you tasted it. With taste as the ultimate test." This familiarity with the sensory aspects of her mother's cooking bred an instinctual key aspect of her own meal preparation because, she explains, "you got to know what it tasted like, how much seasoning you needed because the seasoning was to taste. So that's really how I make the chicken noodle soup that I prepare." Tish recognizes the conundrum faced by followers of all great cooks – capturing the essence that results so closely to that of the originating cook in taste, texture, and tone that the student is pleased with the outcome, and the teacher can sigh with relief. For Tish, "it's difficult to put it into a recipe." So she acknowledges that she must do what her peers who, like her, truly cook from scratch have done for generations: she "will have to make the soup and write down what I am doing as I make the soup to concoct some kind of recipe."

"Even our own taster wanted to know the process that resulted in such a delectable dish."

Knowing what the interviewer is asking, Tish clearly explains, giving details far beyond any recipe, emphasizing certain steps and ingredients, as if words alone will produce its richness and subtle difference from the usual chicken soup. "I made the soup that you received. I made it, implying insight into what it tasted, its difference", continuing the description with an emphasis on the necessary creative care. It has become a recipe-in-retrospect. "It wasn't my quick soup. How it was layered was…I used skinless chicken thighs. I seasoned them like you would fry them and then I didn't batter them, but I put them on a hot skillet with oil and browned them on both sides which helps to seal in the juices and the spices. It was a quick fry and I flipped it over on both sides. I wasn't frying it to cook it. The inside wasn't done… it was half done. Then I took those out of the skillet and let them drain. I sautéed onions, celery, green peppers, carrots in that same grease that I had prepared the chicken in and I used organic chicken stock and I took my pot and I poured the chicken stock in the pot. I kind of shredded the chicken and put it in the pot, put the vegetables in the pot, and seasoned the stock with the Kickin Chicken Finger Likin Seasoning©. I used The Melting Pot's Garlic with Wine. I didn't really add any extra salt because the spice has salt, and I didn't want it to be too salty. I just added flavors… some dried rosemary and some thyme in there. Just let that boil and simmer, that way the chicken finished cooking. I think I used linguine noodles. It was a small pot, probably a 2-quart pot. Once the chicken and the stock were ready and by 'ready' I would mean taste it and if it had enough seasoning then I added the noodles. After adding the noodles, I think I just added the vegetables in there."

If you get the impression that the type of noodles used may vary, you're right. It goes along with the chef who is both familiar and comfortable enough with food and its preparation that the soup recipient chooses.

Her knack for mixing up satisfying soups is a specialty that springs from the example set by her mother who obviously understood the value of comfort food and the power of variety. Growing up with a mother that cooked dinner for the family inspired a ritual that Tish carried on when she had her own family. Even as a working mom, when she arrived home, Tish cooked dinner for her sons. The emphasis on comfort and variety stuck with her. At one point when she really just didn't have time to cook when she got home, she says, "the crockpot was my friend." Tish instilled the importance of home-cooked food in her sons. "I taught my sons how to cook when they were in junior high by taking whatever meat I wanted to have prepared… and they had to call me when they got home from school, so whoever got home first called and I would instruct them how to prepare the meat, and the other son I would instruct on how to do whatever side dish we were gonna have and they would actually end up cooking dinner without realizing that they were really the dinner cooks. So by the time I walked in the house dinner was pretty much finished. They would start cooking around 5 and I would be pulling in about 10 minutes to 6 and dinner would be ready!"

As one who grew up in a family that enjoyed meals together, Tish taught her own boys by carrying on the same dinner tradition. She also remains close to her siblings and misses the warmth and fellowship of their shared table. "It's hard," she laments. Tish describes the way that her family now engenders that recalled sense of togetherness by getting together virtually, using a game app to play over a Zoom connection. During a recent session, the family played bingo using an app her daughter-in-law sent. "There's a lot of fun and we laugh and talk and can see each other." Similarly, during a Zoom call for her birthday, Tish had a slice of cake with some ice cream, and said, "I lit the candle, and they sang happy birthday, and I blew it out. For a family that would normally be together, the virtual gatherings are fun and lively, made so by enjoying a celebratory time despite distance." With this lineage, it's no surprise that Tish's repertoire includes an amazing soup. "Well my mom made homemade soups all the time and I love homemade soup so I will throw together some homemade soup anytime." She keeps ingredients on hand that can be worked into a variety of soups. Her sons inherited the gift of taste, particularly with the soup. Tish describes their well-bred taste, noting that "both sons can tell the difference between me doing it without sautéing everything vs me sautéing everything and they prefer [what they call] 'the long version'", noting that "most times I just think about what I have around here that I can throw in this pot and that is pretty much how I make my soup." As she rattles off just a few possibilities – chicken, vegetable, beef noodle, root vegetable–it becomes clear that she could easily be dubbed, "The Soup Lady." And who knows, for the next get-together, they each may make a pot of chicken noodle soup to enjoy!

In addition to practicing her creative skills with food, Tish is also an accomplished fabric and mixed media artist.

Her
Mixed Media on Canvas

QUICK HEALING CHICKEN NOODLE SOUP

Ingredients

- Kickin Chicken Finger Lickin (spice blend) OR spices of your choice
- Garlic & Wine Seasoning (The Melting Pot spice)
- Black Pepper (Watkins)
- Onion Powder
- Frozen PictSweet Seasoning Blend onion & green peppers (1/2 package)
- Frozen PictSweet Vegetables for Soup
- Olive Oil
- 2 32oz low or no sodium Chicken Broth
- 2 Boneless Skinless Chicken Thighs
- Celery and Celery Tops (1 stalk or use as much or little as you like)
- Angel Hair Pasta (or pasta of your choice) 1 serving amount

Preparation

1. Season & sear chicken in olive oil
2. Add chicken to pot
3. Season and sauté chopped celery & frozen seasoning blend then add to pot
4. Add 2 32ozes of chicken broth to pot and bring pot to a boil
5. Turn down heat to low'med heat and simmer 1 hour
6. Add soup vegetable to pot
7. Cook pasta according to directions add cook pasta to pot
8. Taste and add more seasoning if needed
9. Simmer for 1 hour on low/med heat and ENJOY!!

Jenine Fitzpatrick

THE QUILTING CONNECTION

Chapter Eleven

"I hope to give joy to others that they'll cherish for a long time."
~ Jenine Fitzpatrick

She may not cook, but when Jenine Fitzpatrick "stumbled upon" quilting, its diverse beauty and artistry bumped into the creative edge of this maker of stained glass, dolls, a woman who knit, crocheted and eventually sewed. In addition to her own creative bent, Jenine had witnessed an aunt quilt. So, what seemed coincidental was much more. Attending a summer camp for senior adults that offered an opportunity to join a quilting class brought special memories of her grandmother and gave Jenine "something that connected her to aunt" for advice and fresh conversation, "in addition to just life and family."

Jenine said sewing has been "the one thing that's stuck, and it stuck for several reasons… I just enjoy working with the cloth and then having little pieces together and then this large thing that turns into something really nice." Whether it's the really nice end-product or the pictures of it at various stages, sharing pieces she's working on with an aunt in Chicago provides the novice quilter with advice and suggestions backed by decades of experience. "I think she enjoys it because no one else asks her about quilting, at least in the family. And you know her being in Chicago belongs to a quilting group at church and so they make throws for people in their church or community like a children's home or something like that and they'll get together and make a throw or something like that and so I think… "I know she enjoys when we talk about it. She just lights up and then for me to be able to say, "now how did you do that?" you know to get into the… not just the overall part of the quilt but to say, "now how did you get those two edges there together to make it look so flat?"

Jenine is challenged to improve her craft by the questions, by the energy they share, and the sheer joy that comes from the exchange, "you know just things like that, so I really do think she enjoys it." These conversations hold an added special quality for Jenine, too, since there are no quilters in the family in Jenine's age group or younger. "I enjoy it if she doesn't, I really do," she muses. In their work together, the bond grows, woven into the fabric of their creations threaded tightly with the language of mutual love. "Even though she lives in Chicago I can tell her what problems I run into, and she can give me solutions to think of or another way to solve an issue," Jenine says. She sometimes visits her aunt, taking along pictures of the quilts that she's completed and comparing them to those her aunt has worked on.

A computer programmer by profession, Jenine likens quilting to her work in technology, "putting little pieces together to create the big picture," a process that gives her great joy. From the connection to her aunt and in a different manner, her grandmother, Jenine derives joy and shares that pleasure with others. In a heritage she shares with many quilters in St. Louis, Jenine's grandmother was from a small town in Mississippi. Living several states away, she did not spend time quilting with her grandmother, but like the connection with her aunt, interwoven into Jenine's legacy are stories and vivid memories of her grandmother's love of quilting. She recalls on rare occasions as a small child seeing her grandmother's quilts and witnessing the lively conversations as her grandmother and a group of women worked together, hand sewing a project on a large loom. "I didn't live with her or know a lot about her," Jenine says, but she links these memories to the warm love conveyed in knowing that each of her grandmother's children – including Jenine's own mother – received a quilt that her grandmother made. She laments that "I've asked people in the family if they have a quilt our grandmother did and no one seems to be able to find one," so Jenine has revived the practice of gifting family and special friends with her creations, including many of her cousins and other relatives.

Jenine enjoys the creative expression that quilting affords, but even more so relishes the sharing it inspires and "enjoys more giving [quilts] to other people and seeing them being happy and enjoying it and having something they cherish and a memory for however long." The combination of creativity and giving offers "one thing that I do enjoy" which Jenine describes as "a little piece of me sharing what craft or what gift I have with someone else. I just love to do it and give it to others."

Prompted by this desire to share the joy of a personalized gift, she recently created a t-shirt quilt to commemorate a cousin's college graduation. "I didn't want to give her money or anything like that," opting instead to give "something she can cherish – not only her T-shirts but having them together in something her cousin made." Jenine adds that she hopes to "give joy to others that they'll cherish for a long time."

Tracy Beavers

PREPARING SOMETHING SPECIAL

Chapter Twelve

When you talk with Tracy Beavers, it is very clear what she is passionate about. It is her deep love of, and commitment to, her family including her husband Glenn, her mother, her children, cousins, and other extended family, as well as close friends. She has a big heart and it's full of love.

Her other passion is her professional and service work. Tracy is a businesswoman and community advocate. She is the proud owner of Le Fit bra and shapewear boutique in Old North St Louis. "I've been in that area for about 5 years. It's an up-and-coming community and I'm very excited to be a part of the growth."

As a licensed agent for local health plans in the St. Louis market, Tracy specializes in educating people in her community about Medicare and enrolls them in Medicare health plans. Her love of people and helping others landed her in a position that enables her to serve. "I never thought I would get to this point in my life and I would be so blessed in doing community activities, and just loving it and making a difference. I sincerely think I have made a difference."

She goes on to talk about when we met. To be honest, I hadn't expected her to talk about me during the interview. She said, "And then I met Paulette, Dr. Sankofa…When I first came into North St Louis; she was the first person to welcome me with open arms… you know my family loves her… we sit in my shop many days, especially on many Saturdays. It's kind of special time together. "We talk about wanting to make a difference in the community."

Those Saturday afternoon conversations with Tracy are something that many women in the community share at her retail business. On any given Saturday you might find women gathered to discuss incontinence, for bra fittings, having a "bedazzle your bra" party, or doing something as simple as sitting around talking about politics or other issues facing women. Tracy always has a welcoming, and empowering environment in which women can gather and feel special.

COOKING AND SHARING LOVE IS A FAMILY TRADITION

Cooking is another way Tracy shares love. Between her mother, both grandmothers, and aunts, as well as one of her grandfathers, Tracy was surrounded not simply by cooks, but good cooks.

"So, there was cooking around me and I saw how my family was very passionate about it and they just put all their… thoughts into it… I tell you – you really have to put a thought into cooking." Tracy feels it's nothing that you can just casually do when you say "I'm gonna cook an egg." For her there's preparation that goes into cooking even something as simple as an egg. She says "Because you know if you serve that egg, you are gonna want that egg to taste good." For Tracy, it's all about her caring about people and for her, preparing food is an act of love and caring.

Tracy may not have had opportunities to cook in her younger years, but she didn't miss the subtle and bold nuances in how each of her relatives transferred their passion and thoughts into their dishes and the craft of cooking. "I didn't begin to cook until I became an adult. I mean I like food with lots of taste. In the last 20 years, I got married and I had to cook… it's a regular thing now."

Tracy's mother's chicken wing recipe is a family favorite. Her mom used to cook them when we would travel to Six Flags Amusement Park. And Tracy has four kids so during their trips to Six Flags, her mom always cooked the chicken wings. My baby son would say "We want chicken wings. We want chicken wings." So, her Mom had to prepare the chicken wings. They would look forward to that tradition and even carried it over to make it a Friday night regular event in her home.

Her mother's a little older now, so Tracy has kind of picked up that tradition. Tracy said, "I was like cooking something special, so I wanted to see if I could keep the chicken wig tradition going?"

LET'S TALK ABOUT COOKING!

To be honest, her description of the process of preparing, and cooking chicken wings, shows that for Tracy, it's all in the details and the process. She excitedly, but matter-of-factly rolled off ingredients, steps, and techniques for frying chicken, weaving together a story that melds together an intricate progression of precision and creativity. Even so, she says, "It's my really simple recipe that I got the foundation for from my mother. It's nothing real fancy. but I tell you the seasoning is what makes the wings." She also says "You know preparing in the right grease and skillet or fryer is essential. Let's get started.

Ingredients

> 5 lbs. of chicken wings. I am very particular about my wings. "First of all, I don't like big chicken wings. She says she doesn't like the chicken wings that are very large, So, she has specific stores she goes to in downtown St. Louis at Soulard Market. Soulard is a well-known open-air market. She explains that there are a couple of vendors down there who have small, clean chicken wings.
>
> 4 caps (approximately 4 tsp) of white vinegar
> Enough water to completely cover the wings in a bowl or other container. You will need to do this twice.
>
> Garlic powder, Lowry seasoning salt, and black pepper. The amount you use is up to your taste. I don't personally use heavy seasoning, especially salt.
>
> Wheat flour. Enough to coat the wings and shake in a bag, a few at a time.

Peanut oil. You will need enough to fill your skillet or deep fryer.

Deep fryer or large cast-iron skillet

Tongs or long-handle cooking fork

Draining rack or plate covered with paper towel

Preparation

1. The first thing she does is make sure her work area is prepped and clean. She says "You know, I like a clean kitchen while I cook. If my kitchen isn't clean, I cannot cook. I am a very neat cook."

2. Tracy's preparation process is a combination of tradition, memory, personal touch, and skill. Tracy doesn't want a lot of feathers on the wings, so if you purchasing chicken wings, make sure to find them as clean as possible. "They have a certain look to them. If they don't look right, you probably don't want to purchase them." She usually buys a couple of pounds.

3. When she gets them home, she sorts the wings, because she wants to do her own cleaning. "I like to clean them. I don't want any of the yellow on them, so make sure you clean that yellow off of them. For any remains of the feathers I use vinegar. She takes two caps full of the vinegar added to the bowl with enough water to cover the wings and gives them a thorough wash. Then let she lets them soak for a little while. Not more than 10 minutes. Once she does that, she cleans them again in the same combination of vinegar and water. Finally, she rinses them in lukewarm water.

4. Next, she pats them dry, making sure all the water is off of them, and then puts them on some paper towels. Tracy laughs "That's the day that I am going to use half the roll of paper towels and make sure they are good and dry."

5. Then I spread the wings out and put my seasoning on both sides." I use garlic, I use pepper, and that's about it… I may throw in a little bit of Lawry's seasoning… just a tad, not much…a lot of people now dealing with blood pressure problems and I don't want the chicken to be too salty." Tracy wants to keep things on the healthy side.

6. Then she prepares her flour. "Believe it or not, I use whole wheat flour. I fry my wings in whole wheat flour…"

And there's more…

7. Now it's time to fill the deep-fryer or skillet with the peanut oil. Tracy says "But I'm gonna tell you something, you've got to get a deep fryer, and you have got to have the right one. My daughter invested in me a deep fryer." Tracy says her deep fryer is high-tech, and does all kinds of fancy stuff including spinning around. "Actually, once that's done, I lift them out of the fryer and I tell you, talking about crispy chicken wings!"

8. She shares that you have to eat them when they're hot and coming out of the grease. They are just fantastic. "I'm going to tell you my family eats every one of my chicken wings. They leave and I have no leftovers." Tracy says she loves cooking these special "prepared with love" wings for her family and friends.

Selas Kidane

EATING LIKE HOME: A CELEBRATION OF THE FOOD TRADITIONS OF MY HOMELAND

Chapter Thirteen

My name is Selas Kidane, I'm originally from Eritrea, which is a very diverse country, located in East Africa. Its diversity comes from the many groups of people from surrounding countries that converge in Eritrea bringing with them their cultures. It is bordered to the northeast and east by the Red Sea, Sudan to the west, Ethiopia to the south, and Djibouti to the southeast. Three decades ago, I embarked on a life-altering journey, fleeing my birth-country during the struggle for Eritrean independence. I came into the U.S. as refugee in 1991 and settled in St. Louis. This transition, although fraught with challenges, became the foundation of my profound appreciation for the intrinsic value of traditional foods and the role of nutrition in health and wellness.

As I reminisce about the cultural and nutritional practices of Eritrea, I think about how fasting on Wednesdays and Fridays and the Lenten season dictated our dietary choices. Meals emphasized legumes and vegetables over meat. In Eritrea, the simplicity and nutritional richness of homegrown foods were taken for granted. Eritrean cuisine, rich in vegetables, beans, legumes, wholegrain, including barley, mostly gluten free, such as Teff, sorghum, millet, underscores a tradition of eating that naturally aligns with healthful living and aging well. The traditional preparation of a variety plant-based dishes includes Alicha and Silsi, beans and legume-based dishes, including Hilbet, Timtimo, Shiro, Fulmedamas and so forth. Plant based traditional delicacies reflected a deep-seated respect for food's nutritional and communal value.

The journey to St. Louis introduced me to a vastly different food landscape, marked by accessibility to fast foods and the absence of those fresh, homegrown flavors. Adapting to life in the U.S. presented challenges, especially with the easy availability of processed foods and the busy life that left little room for the labor-intensive cooking practices of my heritage. It is also connected to the social customs of hospitality.

Because my homeland has a rich cultural tapestry, it offers a unique approach to hospitality, especially around food, which is central to its social customs. Our cuisine reflects a blend of east African, north African,

Middle Eastern and even Italian influences, because of Eritrea's history and geographical location.

When it comes to hospitality, several customs stand out, showcasing the warmth and communal spirit of the Eritrean people. One of the most symbolic traditions of Eritrean hospitality is the coffee ceremony. Coffee, or 'bun' in Tigrinya (one of the languages spoken in Eritrea), is not just a beverage but a significant cultural ritual. The ceremony involves roasting fresh green coffee beans, grinding them, and then brewing the coffee in a clay pot called a 'jebena.' The process is aromatic and sensory, often performed when welcoming guests. It's a sign of respect and friendship to participate in this ritual, and it's customary to stay for at least three rounds of coffee, symbolizing the progression from acquaintance to friendship.

Sharing meals is also a cherished custom. In Eritrea, meals are typically shared from a single large plate, emphasizing unity and equality among diners. The most common dish is injera, a sourdough-rise flatbread with a unique, slightly spongy texture, served with various stews (tsebhi). Diners use pieces of injera to scoop up the stews, eating with their hands, which is a communal and bonding experience. Offering the best morsels to guests is a sign of respect and care.

Another common practice of our culture, is inviting guests for meals. I cherish that and it reflects the open-heartedness and generosity of Eritrean culture. It's typical for hosts to insist on guests eating more, as a way of showing hospitality and ensuring that guests are well-fed and satisfied. Refusing food is not considered polite; hence, guests are encouraged to accept the hospitality graciously. In many ways it's a lot like Black cultural traditions around hospitality I have found since moving here.

Then, there is a cherished practice in my culture of serving elders first. It is a key aspect of Eritrean food etiquette, showing respect and honor. In a group setting, the eldest are given priority, both in serving and in starting the meal. This respect for age and hierarchy underscores the communal and intergenerational bonds within Eritrean society.

My story is not just about my personal journey and memories, it has been a catalyst for personal health, and also about the broader implications of diet on community wellness in my new home, in St. Louis. The alarming prevalence of health issues like high blood pressure and diabetes within the Black diaspora starkly contrasts with the virtually nonexistent rates of these conditions among older generations in Eritrea, who lived on unprocessed, homegrown foods.

This acknowledgement of the change in eating patterns of people moving from rural areas to big cities, is very close to the changes I witnessed for myself as an immigrant. That stark contrast became a turning point, igniting a passion for nutrition and a return to the roots of my traditional eating habits. In addition, my struggle with health issues like acid reflux, prompted a deeper exploration into nutrition, reinforcing the belief in the benefits of traditional, homemade meals over processed alternatives.

This realization spurred my journey of discovery, learning about the nutritional differences between the unrefined grains of Eritrea and the refined alternatives found abroad. It was a lesson in the importance of understanding what goes into our bodies and the long-term effects of our dietary choices.

Now, balancing a demanding schedule with the commitment to traditional cooking, I began to advocate for a mindful approach to eating. It's about respecting the body by choosing wholesome, nutritious foods and understanding the impact of diet on aging and health. I encourage others to embrace change, however challenging it may be, to benefit from a nutritionally rich diet that can significantly enhance quality of life.

Through my journey, I continue to strive to maintain a positive outlook, viewing dietary choices as a means to a healthier, more fulfilled life. Yet, I recognize change might not come over night. I think in part, my success is a testament to the power of tradition, the importance of nutrition, and my unbreakable spirit. I believe the same can happen for you when you seek to make a difference in your life.

EXPLORE HEALTHY NUTRITIONAL ALTERNATIVES TO SUPPORT HEALTHY AGING

Vegan (plant-based) cuisine offers many options with a wealth of benefits. Plant-based nutrition is rich in fruits, vegetables, legumes, wholegrains, nuts, and seeds, and provides a diverse array of nutrients, essential vitamins and minerals.

Plant-based foods are high in dietary fiber, vitamins, A, C, E, K, folate, magnesium, unsaturated fat, and countless phytochemicals. These nutrients contribute to improved heart health, reduced risk of chronic diseases, lower blood pressure, and better digestive health.

In addition, plant-based nutrition helps maintain healthy weight, because they are lower in calories, and contain healthy fat. Also, studies have shown that a vegan's diet has a lower risk of developing heart disease, type 2 diabetes, hypertension, certain cancers, and obesity. The high fiber, antioxidant, and phytonutrient content of plant-based foods play a significant role in this protective effect.

I have developed a program that you can follow on YouTube, Vegeatrea (https://www.youtube.com/@VEGEATREA). My goal is to promote universal healing through plant nutrition, beyond tradition, by combining healthy traditional ingredients, with modified food preparation techniques to make home cooking less intimidating and further enhance nutritional value that meet today's demand for healthy diet that helped me restore my health and maintain healthy weight the natural way. Join VEGEATREA for receipt of videos.

Selas Kidane is originally from Eritrea, which is located in Horn of East Africa, known as the Red Sea State. She is a passionate healthy food developer and is part of VEGEATREA YouTube channel https://www.youtube.com/@VEGEATREA. This channel was designed to promote healthy eating and harmony through the art of food and culture. She studied at St. Louis Community College, where she earned her Associate degree in accounting, and is currently studying for a bachelor's degree in leadership and management.

Selas is a full time employee, working in accounting field. *"I love working with numbers, but my true passion is culinary art and I enjoy researching about other cultures."* She has been a volunteer African Heritage & Health Ambassador for A Taste of African Heritage (ATOAH), teaching seven sessions between 2014 and 2019. including large seminars on Oldways African Heritage Diet, a nonprofit origination that research food and culture. Selas is one of the contributing authors on OASIS: OLDWAYS "AFRICANA SOUP IN STORIES."

"I'm passionate about culinary arts that are a reflection of my Eritrean cultural heritage, which is a blessing I inherited from my family."

Paulette Sankofa

I AM WEAVING THE COLORFUL THREADS OF MY LIFE THROUGH FABRIC ART AND CUISINE

Chapter Fourteen

"I am Weaving the Colorful Threads of My Life through Fabric Art and Cuisine" is a deeply personal and introspective statement that suggests I use quilting/fabric art and cuisine as a means of storytelling and self-expression. For me these creative endeavors are not just hobbies, but integral parts of my life journey. They reflect my experiences, memories, aspirations, and have been a part of curating the stories in St. Louis Black Women's Quilting and Cuisine: Stories of Love and Hope.

As a shared meal nourishes the body, so a quilt, passed from generation to generation, warms and nourishes the spirit. Both recipes and quilts preserve the culture and history of a people and their social, historic, and artistic connections to their past and their future.

~ The Black Family Dinner Quilt Cookbook

I am a fabric artist, and one who has explored many types of cuisine. At one time I was in the Culinary Arts program at the Adams Mark Hotel until I sustained a life changing back injury while working. I also worked at Café' de France, a boutique French restaurant that was located in downtown St. Louis.

I grew up learning to cook at a very early age. I would watch my mother cook on a regular basis, but my father was also very good in the kitchen. I baked my first cake, from scratch, at five years of age. I wasn't allowed to use my mother's Sunbeam mixer at that age, so I had to stir everything by hand. That meant using one of her wooden spoons. I still remember my mother talking about the importance of wooden spoons. She had a number of them in different shapes and sizes. Wooden spoons held an important place in our household when I was growing up.

Fast forward a few years, when my mother was living in Indiana. She was part of a Black Elder women's group I started called The Wise Women. The group published a small cookbook called **"Every Woman**

Should Have a Wooden Spoon". Well you know who heavily influenced the selection of that title. Yes, my Mom. One of the things she contributed was the following poem.

The Wooden Spoon, a Poem
~ Pinkie Luella Handley

Now if I had a chance to fly in space, I would like to fly to the moon. And I would not leave my earthly treasure, that is my precious wooden spoon.
When I was a little girl growing up, I used to watch my mother cook. Sometimes she would cook from experience, and sometime she would cook from a book.
And it was just a pleasure, to play around the room. It was there that I learned my lesson very early, that every kitchen should have a wooden spoon.
Now every woman that has a kitchen, or hopes to have one soon. So, please remember that every kitchen should always have a wooden spoon.
This special utensil is a very useful thing 'cause it beats, it stirs, it measures, it tastes, it even plays a tune. That is why it is so important that every kitchen must have a wooden spoon.
Now the wooden spoon came before the metal spoon, and other utensils we buy. So the wooden spoon has been around for a very long time. And it's use, well it will not die soon, because every kitchen should have a wooden spoon.

Years later I moved to Minnesota, and one day walked into Heaven High African Gallery. I'm not sure how the conversation got started, but somehow we started to talk about my love for cooking and wooden spoons. The shop owner, Adeyemi Chaka said "Wait just a minute. I have something to show you." He went to the back gallery and returned with a tall, elegant wooden sculpture of a woman holding a wooden spoon. I was blown away. He told me that I was meant to own it. I asked him the price, and while I really wanted to purchase it, I couldn't fit it in my budget at the time. I had just returned to graduate school fulltime. I will never forget what he said next. He said, "Not a problem my Sister. You take her home and I have no doubt you will pay me when you can. I want you to own this woman with a wooden spoon". Chaka was right. I paid him as soon as possible, and we have remained dear friends ever since.

Not long after acquiring her I did some research on the cultural significance of the wooden spoon in many African cultures. For instance, among the Senufo culture, particularly among women, these spoons are not merely utilitarian objects but are imbued with spiritual and social meaning. In Senufo culture, a beautifully carved wooden spoon is a representation of prestige and symbolizes a woman's hospitality and generosity. It signifies her willingness to share her resources and home with others, earning her high respect in the community. Those qualities were definitely valued our home, and in my mother's way of relating to others.

The wooden spoon definitely held significance with my mother, and it has been carried on through me. The Woman with the Wooden Spoon sculpture still graces my home.

EVERY WOMAN SHOULD HAVE A WOODEN SPOON AND LOTS OF FABRIC

I grew up in a household, and community, with lots of women who were fabric creatives. My mother worked in the garment industry in St. Louis. They made clothing for Worths, SAKS Fifth Avenue, and other women's clothing retailers. She was able to purchase fabric from leftover products and that meant I had beautiful skirts, blouses, and all other types of items. One thing I remember she engrained in me was to always buy natural fabrics like silk, cotton, or wool, and I could always know if it is real if moths eat it. I never forgot, and still try to follow that rule today.

I was also heavily influenced by my Aunt Irene, who was my mother's older sister. She lived right across the alley from us at the time. I loved to go over to her house because not only was she fun to be around, but she also let me watch her sew and taught me little techniques. The biggest thrill was being allowed to play in the mounds of fabric in her place. Oh my goodness, it seemed like mountains of all types of fabric in a never ending selection of colors, and textures.

She would allow me to have scraps and make little creations from them. Nothing I made was ever a mistake. The more I added to my creations, the more fabric, buttons, and other embellishments she gave me to add on. I think that was the beginning of what would later become my passion in other expressions of fabric in art.

My interest in quilts came out of my love of fabric, and experience with a very kind neighbor. In 1985, was living in an apartment in St. Louis and I had decided to relocate to Chicago later that year. I told my older, upstairs neighbor about my plans and she explained to me that it gets really, really cold in Chicago. She went on to say that before I would be leaving, she would have a gift for me.

One day, about a month before I was to leave, she invited me upstairs for dinner and showed me what she was working on. Laid out on her bed was a quilt. She had been hand sewing this absolutely wonderful work of art. The design, I later found out was bear paws. But she used no pattern that she had to cut around. It was all her skill that she had learned from someone else. The thing that struck me most was that she cared enough to make the quilt for me. I still have the quilt, though well worn, 39 years later.

THROUGH A LENS OF COLORFUL THREADS

I use the metaphor of colorful threads because that's the way I see, and sense the world. For me, the world is an enlivening vibration of the colors, and sounds, and smells, and all of the amazing textures. It's the way that the food and fabric speak to me and tells me what it wants to be. I have so much joy in creating food and fabric items that I can share with others. I want the recipients of my creations to experience what I felt the first time I saw the Nigerian bronze art exhibit in Atlanta over forty years ago. I was awestruck by the magnificent bronze sculptures and intricately detailed jewelry. I want people to experience what I felt when I first saw the painting The Water Lilies by Claude Monet. My spirit just soared and I began to weep.

It's always my hope that what I create will touch someone, and that they will have a spiritual experience from it. We just sometimes overlook those experiences. Take time to connect with the meals prepared with love. Embrace the love put into a gift from another person. There are opportunities all around us to find the spirit in expressions of creativity.

Paulette Sankofa as Chef

PEANUT BUTTER AND CURRY CHICKEN WITH VEGETABLES

Ingredients

- 2 bell peppers
- 4 Carrots chopped to 1 inch
- 2 large sweet onions
- 2 cups of broccoli
- 2 cups cauliflower
- 1 cup snow peas
- 1 cup bean sprouts
- 1 can coconut milk
- 1 tbsp. sesame oil
- 3 tbsp. olive oil
- ¼ cup natural chunky peanut butter
- 2 cups of protein; either chicken, cod fish, or seafood. Leave the fish in approximately 4 inch filets
- 1 tbsp. powdered or 1 inch fresh sliced ginger
- ½ tsp. chili flakes
- 1 heaping tbsp. curry powder
- 1 heaping tbsp. tomato paste
- ½ tsp. salt

Preparation

1. Sauté bell peppers, carrots, and onions in oils
2. Push veggies to the side and add protein
3. Cook covered for about 8-10 minutes until protein is done. Turn over as needed
4. Add tomato paste, peanut butter, and coconut milk. Mix together.
5. Add remaining veggies, ginger, chili flakes, and salt
6. Cover and simmer for 10 minutes
7. Serve over Basmati or Jasmine rice

SENEGALESE FISH AND ONIONS
My Version (lower sodium)

Ingredients
- 2 pounds Cod filets or jack salmon
- 4 large sweet onions sliced across
- 1 can fire roasted tomatoes
- 2 cloves of garlic minced
- 1 tbsp. mustard preferably Dijon
- ½ tsp. black pepper
- 4 tbsp. olive oil
- 4 tsp unsalted butter
- ½ tsp. salt

Preparation
1. Heat oil, salt, and butter in a sauté pan
2. When butter melts, add sliced onion. Sauté onions and garlic on low-ish heat for approximately 40 minutes until onions soften and caramelize
3. Lay fish on top of onions, add tomatoes, and black pepper
4. Cover and simmer at a medium heat for approximately 20 minutes until fish is cooked and sauce formed

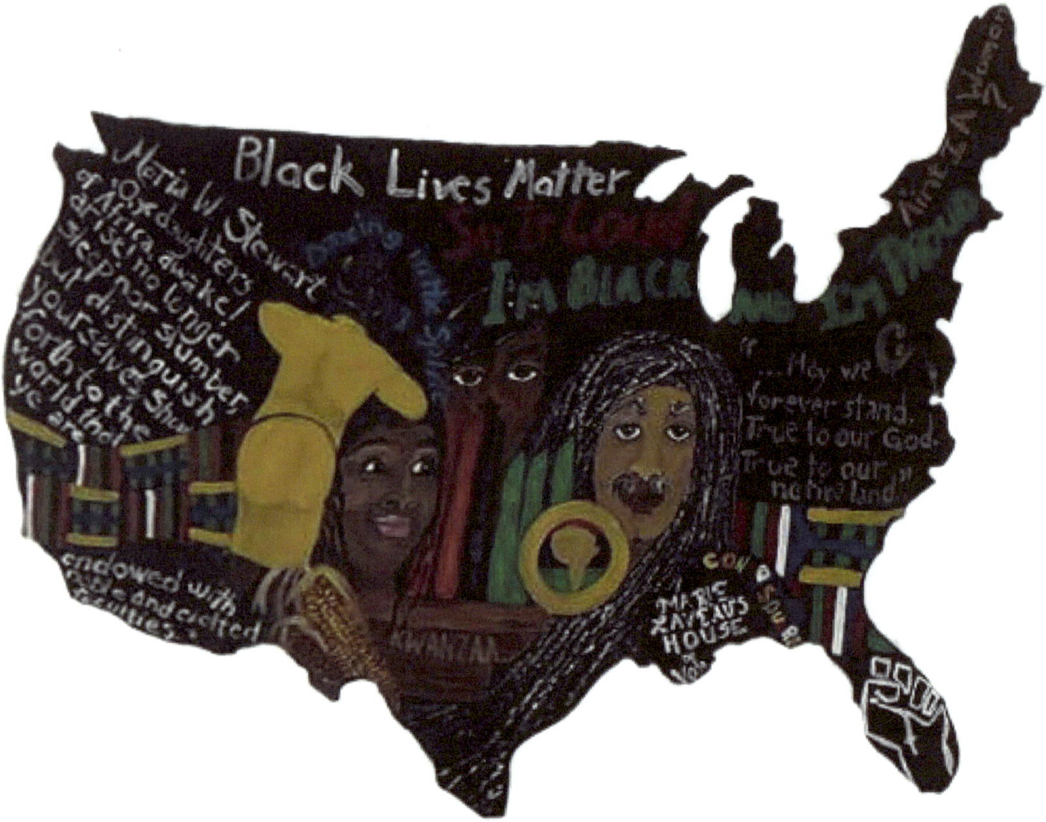
Black Lives Matter
Maria W. Stewart
O ye daughters of Africa, awake! arise! no longer sleep nor slumber but distinguish yourselves. Show forth to the world that ye are
endowed with noble and exalted faculties.
I'M BLACK AND I'M PROUD
Ain't I A Woman?
"...May we forever stand. True to our God. True to our native land."
MARIE LAVEAU'S HOUSE
KWANZAA

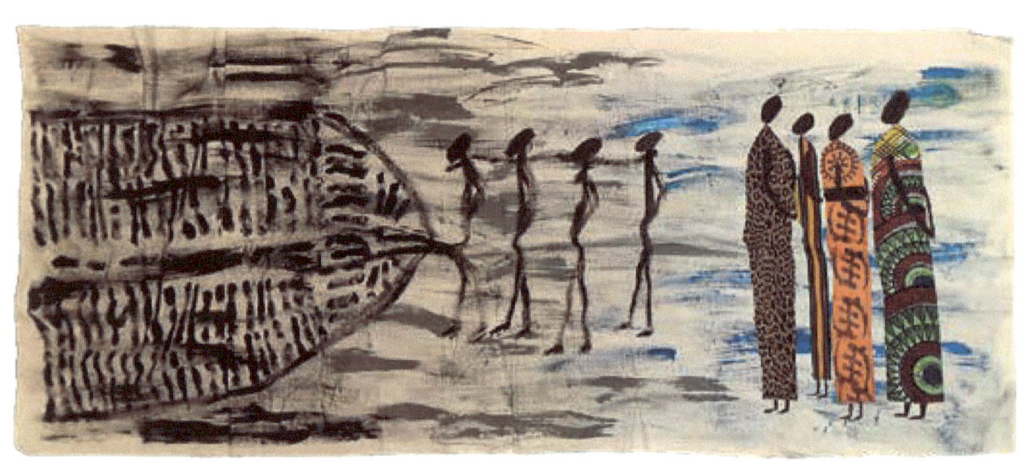

Collecting Memories

NOW IT'S YOUR TURN!

Chapter Fifteen

Collecting stories from your family or community can be a meaningful and enriching experience, fostering connections and preserving valuable memories.

Here are a few ideas to get you started...

DEFINE YOUR PURPOSE: Clarify why you want to collect these stories. Are you interested in preserving family history, documenting cultural traditions, or simply fostering a sense of connection? Having a clear purpose will guide your efforts. For example, in writing this book, I wanted to gather stories of Black St. Louis women who weren't necessarily public figures, but who had stories to tell that others could appreciate and relate to.

_____

_____

_____

_____

IDENTIFY YOUR AUDIENCE: Determine who you want to collect stories from. This could include immediate family members, extended relatives, neighbors, or other members of your community. For example, your audience might be your family at this time, and will also be shared in generations yet unborn.

_____

_____

_____

_____

CHOOSE COLLECTION METHODS: Decide how you'll gather stories. Options include informal conversations, structured interviews, written submissions, oral histories, storytelling events, digital platforms, saving photos or samples of memorable items such as letter, quilts, pieces of clothing, or a combination of these approaches. For example, I saved my father's Pullman Porter uniforms, his timesheets, and 26 years of postcards he wrote to my mother.

_____

_____

_____

_____

PLAN YOUR APPROACH: Consider the best way to approach potential storytellers. Choose settings and times conducive to open and comfortable conversations, and be respectful of people's schedules and preferences. For example, you might approach people individually. Or you might create a group invitation allowing people to schedule a time. Be sure to have details available for people, and try to anticipate potential questions. As far as locations, you might choose to meet with them in their homes where they or comfortable, or in a room at your local library. You will need a place where there are few distractions. Also, your method of collecting stories will dictate your location.

_____
_____
_____
_____

CONDUCTING CONVERSATIONS OR INTERVIEWS

When collecting stories through conversations or interviews, it's important to ask open-ended questions that encourage storytelling and reflection. Here are some examples:

Family Background:
- Can you share some stories about our family's origins or early history?
- What were our ancestors like, and what values did they pass down to us?

_____
_____
_____
_____

Memorable Events:
- What are some significant events or milestones in our family's history?
- Can you recall any particularly memorable family gatherings or celebrations?

_____
_____
_____
_____

Family or Community Traditions:
- Family or Community Traditions:
- What are some traditions or rituals that have been passed down through the generations in our family?
- How have these traditions evolved over time, and why are they important to us?

_____
_____
_____
_____

Personal Memories:
- What are some of your fondest childhood memories or experiences growing up in our family or community?
- Can you share any stories about challenges or obstacles our family has overcome together?
- Are there challenges that have been faced by our family?

_____
_____
_____
_____

Life Lessons:
- What wisdom or life lessons have you learned from your family or community elders?
- Are there any stories or anecdotes that have had a significant impact on your life or the way you see the world?

RECORDING AND PRESERVING

Document Conversations: Record conversations or interviews (with permission) using audio, video, or written notes to capture the stories accurately. Consider Zoom, Google Docs or other methods. You might even consider making a series of Facebook or Instagram reels. Or you might create a YouTube channel.

Respect Privacy: Respect Privacy: Be mindful of sensitive information and obtain consent from storytellers regarding the use and dissemination of their stories. This is particularly important if you choose to use social media or other methods that have a digital footprint.

Archive and Share: Create a family archive or digital repository to preserve collected stories for future generations. Consider sharing these stories through family reunions, gatherings, newsletters, social media, or other platforms.

Encourage Participation: Encourage other family members or community members to participate in the storytelling process by sharing their own memories and experiences, fostering a sense of collective ownership and engagement.

_____
_____
_____
_____

By following these steps and asking thoughtful questions, you can effectively collect and preserve stories that reflect the rich tapestry of experiences and memories within your family or community, strengthening bonds and honoring heritage.

ADDITIONAL NOTES

_____
_____
_____
_____
_____
_____
_____
_____
_____
_____
_____
_____
_____
_____

ADDITIONAL NOTES

www.ingramcontent.com/pod-product-compliance
Lightning Source LLC
Chambersburg PA
CBHW041609220426
43667CB00001B/12